Your Way is Not God's Way

By: George A. Hafley

xulon
PRESS

Copyright © 2008 by George A. Hafley

Your Way is Not God's Way
by George A. Hafley

Printed in the United States of America

ISBN 978-1-60647-180-7

All rights reserved solely by the author. The author guarantees all contents are original and do not infringe upon the legal rights of any other person or work. No part of this book may be reproduced in any form without the permission of the author. The views expressed in this book are not necessarily those of the publisher.

Unless otherwise indicated, Bible quotations are taken from The King James Version of the Bible. Copyright © 1984, 1977 by Thomas Nelson Inc.

I would like to dedicate this book to my sister, Sylvia Kindelberger. For all the many, many hours spent and for all the help, support and dedication she has shown me, throughout the writing of this book. Without <u>her</u> help, this book would not have been published.

                    Thank You and May God Bless You, Sis!!!

www.xulonpress.com

Your Way is Not God's Way
By: George A. Hafley

Chapter 1

If there's one thing I have learned in life, it's to obey God's spoken Word, when He speaks to you. The Lord has dealt with me for the last three weeks, concerning writing this book. I have no idea how to start or how it's going to end. But I will trust and obey His Word. So, here we go…

Let, me start by saying a little bit about myself. I was born June 6,1956 on an Naval Base, in Landstuhl, Germany. I have two other brothers and five sisters, eight of us in the litter! Our dad was in the United States Air Force for, twenty years. He was a Christian man, he never drank, smoked or anything of that matter. He was a faithful man of God and a regular Church going man.

As a young man, our dad planted the seed of God into all of his children. We all went to Church on a regular basis. Dad, has since went to live with the Lord, he passed away on March 5,1997 he lived his whole life, to someday be with our, Savior. Looking back on my life, I have to say, "this was one of the best things our dad had done, for all of us kids, and that was planting the seed of Christ into our lives." Without this up bringing, I know, I would have been dead along time ago.

The Lord has plans for our lives if only we allow Him to do so. If not, the Devil will take over our lives. Believe me, if you don't believe the truth then you will believe a lie. Who are you going to believe in?

The single most urgent problem you face as a Christian believer isn't whether you're going to Heaven when you die. You know, in your inner self that your faith, is in Jesus Christ of Nazareth, who received you into His Kingdom, guarantees your eternal destiny will be with God. Death, holds no fear for you. It's only a transition to a greater life that God has for you.

The most urgent problem is how to get your needs met, while you live here on this earth, on your way to Heaven, spiritually, physically, and financially as you witness for Christ and carry on His work. Our needs, change from time to time, but, a fact of life is that when one need is met, another need presents itself. We're never without a need. Your needs challenges your walk with the Lord. It takes your ability to get along in life successfully,and tries to hide God from your life. It'll fill you with anxiety and fear. It creates doubts, that questions, if you are saved? If God, really cares about your existence here on earth, if you can make it in a world filled with disbelief, cursed with sickness, and disease, which defies you, everyday of your life. In, whatever form, spiritually, physically or financially isn't being met in a way that gives you some breathing room, some peace of mind, some evidence that you are going to make it, there is a great feeling of wanting to give up. Frustration comes up inside of you, because the need just won't go away. Why has this happened to me? What have I done to deserve this? All these questions, often unanswerable, will increase your frustration of, "Why me?" Is there something wrong with me? This is when Satan, slips in and begins to insinuate that being born again, isn't so great, walking with the Lord doesn't pay. Many people, who don't even believe in the Lord, are getting along better than you are, your prayers are not being answered, so where's God? Not a great place to be at. Satan just loves to see you in this shape. You cry, why doesn't the Devil just leave me alone? You open your Bible, to do what a good and faithful Christian should do, and read and study the Bible and let God speak to you from His Holy Word. You read, the Bible, but you wonder what it means. You read,the Bible, where all these things had happened back there thousands of years ago, to people you question as being a real person like yourself.

This saith the Lord, "do this and things will work out for you," even if God has to give you a miracle. God, help me please! This is the world we live in, not the Heaven we are going to someday very, very soon. Down, here is where we all hurt, where we lack money, health, hope and friends. Down here, is where the battle is. Here's, where the struggle never stops. This is the real world.

Is there an answer? Yes, there is an answer. The Word of God is as close as, you reaching out and picking it up and opening it and looking up those scriptures that speaks directly to you at the point of your need.

Chapter 2

~~~~~~~

The three key principals of *"faith seed giving"* are so simple and they work if you only, want them to work, by taking a step of faith, beginning right, now. God is so real and He means exactly what He says in, (Philippians 4:19) "My God shall supply all your needs according to His riches in Glory, by Christ Jesus." You must, and you can, if, your will to do it, is there. Believe in your heart the God, I'm talking about exists. He's, at work on this earth; he's rewarded, when you seek Him with your whole heart. He'll multiply the seeds of faith, you sow and He'll give you miracles after miracles, so you can say. "Greater is He who is in me that Satan who is in the world." In, (l John 4:4) it says, "Listen with your heart to what I am saying. I know that here on earth, while you are on your way to Heaven, you will discover God's way, to meet your needs time after time. The whole Bible is just full of rewards from God.

    Faith is something not seen, but is believed in one's heart. Faith seed giving is just like a farmer. He plants a seed, waits for a little while, and then he gets a harvest. When you give, out of faith, on something you don't have, God will give you a harvest. Expect it, for it will come. God's not going to ask you for something you can't give. When He releases His blessings from Heaven, He will bless you ten fold. A weed, can only grow when someone doesn't plant a good seed in a pot of soil. If someone had planted a good seed, one that will bear fruit, something useful or beautiful for our lives, a weed couldn't grow in that spot. In the Bible, there are 58 faith seed blessings. Blessing for every need in your life. Give and it shall be given into you. For sowing a faith seed gift, for a desired result. Your seed will be multiplied. God works with your faith.

Let me witness to you about a $20.00 faith seed gift. On September 21, 2006, I lost my job of six years. It was classified as an unlawful discharge from my job. (I have to call it a devil shop.) Believe me, my whole world came to a complete stop, that day. It was a factory, that packed and shipped car parts, all over the world. The management was very, deceitful. For you see, if there's hate in one's heart, that's what comes out, if you have love in your heart, then that's what comes out, love! I was completely dumbfounded, worried, lost as what to do next. I was scared. I, really didn't know what I was going to do.

On October 20, 2006, a Sunday, I was watching Daystar, a Christian channel. The Sustar ministries, the sermon was about "Flames of Revival." Throughout the sermon, the preacher kept saying, "Whatever your need is, call and plant a faith seed gift, the amount of the gift was up to the Lord and yourself." I must say, "that the Lord whispers, He never screams." We must remain still for Him to talk to us. The sermon was about over, and the Lord spoke to me and said, "George, call right now, and send $20.00 do it now." I, obeyed and called the phone number that was on the T.V. screen. I told the operator, what the Lord wanted me to do. I got their address, and they got mine. They said, "they're going to send me some prayer cloths, and to follow the instructions on the inside of the envelope." The next day was Monday, the very first thing I did was write a check for $20.00 as a faith seed gift and got it in the mail. I knew it was the Lord speaking to my heart. I didn't even have $20.00 in my checking account. I obeyed the Lord anyway. Delayed obedience, becomes disobedience.

On the lower left hand corner of the check where it says, "memo" I wrote "*faith seed gift, job, lawyer, and unemployment*," in Jesus name. I wrote the check and mailed it. That Friday, a letter came from the Sustar Ministries, in Phoenix, Arizona. There were 2 prayer clothes inside, one, I prayed over it and put it inside of my wallet. And the other one, I had to write my name on it, and fill out my prayer request and send it back to them.

I went to the unemployment office and I was denied benefits. Then on, November 17, 2006, I had a second telephone interview, for my unemployment and I didn't have a lawyer. When we obey the good Lord, He rewards us. Now remember, I sent my

Your Way is Not God's Way

faith seed gift on October 16, 2006. Here come the blessings.

Two weeks later, I got one of the best lawyers, he works in, Employment Law. God, helped me to get my unemployment checks. One week, after that I received two checks, one for $1,550 and another for $775.00. I'm telling you, I almost fell out of the chair, that I was sitting on. I shouted a couple times, "*Thank you Jesus, Thank you Jesus!*" I give the Lord all the praise and glory, and that's just the beginning. First, I got my lawyer, then my checks,

I had a $2,000 hospital bill, that I couldn't pay. I made one phone call, to the billing department at the hospital. Later, they sent me a letter stating that my bill had been paid in the full.

I, now have a lawsuit against my former employer. I don't know what the harvest will be on this law suit, but I'll tell you this,"our Heavenly Father in Heaven knows." I believe all of this happened, when I obeyed the Lord with the $20.00 faith seed gift. It's Amazing! I tell you, just Amazing. Here's the strangest part of it all, I didn't have the money in the bank, I wrote the check anyway and the check cleared. To this day, I don't know how it cleared, but it did.

When, we obey God, He will bless us, this I know. Before, any of this happened, I got on my knees in my T.V. room and had a heart to heart prayer with the Lord. I left it at the Lord's feet, I got up and claimed the Victory, from that moment on, I knew in my heart I was going to win. We do, have Victory in Jesus. My wife, Cathy, family and friends were just overwhelmed at what the Lord had done for us. When the

Lord is in the mix, nothing can get in the way of His work.

One thing, I had forgotten to mention, before all of this, I was in a very bad state of depression, I just wanted to die. I felt like I couldn't go on, because the hurt inside of me was so great, I couldn't handle it. I didn't know what to do. I had never had depression in the past. I prayed to our God in Heaven, and I meant every word of it. I prayed, "God, take this awful depression away, I can't handle it anymore." In the name of Jesus, brothers and sisters in Christ. "God healed me instantly, He took the depression away, right then and there!" I prayed, faith believing, that God would help me. I didn't take any pills, and I had no counseling, or hospitalization. *Instantly*, I was healed, "Thank You Jesus!" It was a hurt on the inside that I never, want to experience again. I, give our Heavenly Father in Heaven, all the praise and Glory. For you see, there's power in the blessings, of each prayer. Sit still and listen to God when He speaks to you. Find a closet or room, *anywhere*, you can daily talk to God, He loves to help His people.

You *have not*, because, you *ask not*. When you become partners with God, things in your life will start happening. Anything, God touches, He changes. What you do for others, God will also, do for you.

Chapter 3

How, do you release your faith, through a point of contact with God? You know, wouldn't it be wonderful if faith, could be put into a bottle? If you felt like you needed more faith, you could just go to the store and buy a bottle of it. You're right, it would be wonderful, but you would still have to figure out, how to get the faith, out of the bottle and up to the Lord. "Why, you ask? Well, faith isn't going to do you much good if it's in a bottle or if it's lying dormant in your heart. Faith has to connect with God before it can make a difference in your life.

One of the most powerful ways that I know of, to help you get your faith connected with the Lord, is through a point of contact. Now, a point of contact is something you do, and when you do it, you release your faith to God. It, also helps set the time and place for your miracle to begin. A point of contact is a faith builder, and a hope builder. It's like saying to someone,"the situation on it's own, may seem hopeless, but now, let's believe that God can make a way for a, miracle." A point of contact is something you do, and when you do it, you release your faith. You have to look up to God's power in Heaven. A point of contact can help you turn the switch of faith, on.

God's power, is what helps us. Prayer can help you release your faith so you can touch God's power. Oh yes, your faith, has to be released before it can produce results. It has to come out of, you. It has to become an act of your believing. In (James 2:17) it says, "Faith without works is dead." In other words, as long as your faith, is lying dormant in your heart, it's not going to do you much good. The kind of faith that can produce miracles, is "live faith" that has some action to it, faith that's going up to God. That's what I did with the prayer cloth from the Sunstar Ministries. That was my point of contact. I listen to God's Word, obeyed, and sent the prayer cloth back to them and God did the rest. What a mighty, powerful God we serve! I've had some close friends, but God is my, best friend. You know, I can call on Him anytime, day or night. He even has a toll free number *1-800-U-ASK God*, His phone is never busy, and no one is on the line to say, "Please wait, all lines are busy." Or, "Your call is very important to us." Ten minutes later nothing. With God, it's a direct call, it's never, busy. Thank You Jesus! One line, direct to our God in Heaven. He's there to supply our every need.

God uses many different points of contact. Such as, a prayer, a seed that you sew, a healing touch, a verse from the Bible or a word you receive from the Lord. It could also be a prayer cloth, anointed with oil, A Holy Communion, a letter someone writes to you, or a prayer that you pray for someone, else. Let me list four things, as a point of contact that will help you:

1-Focus your faith on God.
2-Set a time and place for your miracle to begin.
3-Turn loose of all your doubts.
4-Release your faith to the Lord.

If you're facing some kind of problems or struggles, you can release your faith and let it go to God, through a point of contact. Let, me pray for you today, and let my prayer be your point of contact. Let's begin by saying,"Faith, get up to God, and hold on to what you believe, until the answer comes." Let's pray,"Heavenly Father, in the mighty name of Jesus, I come to you today asking, for a miracle. Friends, I pray for you all, to set a time and place for your miracle to begin right now, in the name of Jesus. As, you let your faith go up to God, I pray for His healing power to touch you from the tip of your head to the bottom of your feet. I pray, for the trials that have tried to bring you down, and for you to feel the power of the Lord lifting them off of you and removing them from your life. I believe those problems won't rule over you anymore. In the precious name of Jesus, I pray, we expect a miracle, right now! We claim the Victory." Amen and Amen.

Chapter 4

❦

You know, God expands Himself through us and our giving. Have you ever stopped to think about that? After we're saved by the shedded blood of His Son at Calvary, we're filled with God's Holy Spirit. That means, that we have extended God's Spirit on this earth through one more life. We have extended God's influence in the world. We're one more witness of God's power and love. God's essential nature the primary element of His personality, is that He loves us so much He gives. In (John 3:16) it says, "For God as loved the world, that He gave His only begotten Son, that whosoever believeth in Him should not perish, but will have ever lasting life." So, as you can see the God's-kind, is loving, giving, and receiving. Consider, that, as God's nature, to be our essential nature too, that we can begin loving, giving and receiving, like God does. We too, love that we give. Now, God's-kind of giving isn't a one way street. God gives and keeps on giving.

Our God, also receives and always will, as a result of His giving. It's His giving, that generates what He receives. The seeds that God sews, come back to Him in harvest, of our Salvation, the recovering of our lives, that have been stolen away by Satan. When God gets us back, that's the two way street of giving and receiving, of sewing and reaping, and then the harvest, that our God, is engaged 24/7.

Jesus, reminds us that when we're a sinner, and then recognizes that God's gift of Salvation, is offered freely, to us and repents and then we're, saved. There's joy among the Angles in Heaven, over one sinner that repents. In (Luke 15:7) it says, "I say unto you, that likewise joy shall be in Heaven over one sinner that repenteth, more than over ninety and nine just persons, which need no repentance." *Wow!!!* You're actually dealing with God Himself, when you give, to further His work here, on this earth.

God alone, determines which men, He chooses to give back to you. They may not be, and usually aren't the ones, that we would choose, but the men God chooses, will go out of their way, if need be, to help you as God has promised. We, must obey God whether we like it or not. I just love the way God does things. I know God allows us to go through bad times, so we can become stronger in, Him. He'll use our bad times and turn them into blessed time, to help other people, in there time of trouble.

In (Luke 6:38) it says, "Give and it shall be given into you good measure, pressed down, and shaken together and running over, shall men give into your bosom. For with the same measure that ye mete withal it shall be measured to you again." It thrills me that in the final analysis, God is in control of what we give, the seeds we plant, and the harvest we receive. Many, people may give to you, without realizing it, or just why they're doing it, or what they are doing. But, now you know. God has the harvest under control. God is doing and multiplying. God is measuring out to you, His rewards.

Have you ever felt like you were out of options? Let me give you a story from the Bible that will speak directly to you when you feel this way. In (Judges 14-16) it says, We have the story of Samson, who had everything going for him. Then, he disobeyed God and he lost his power, and got into a bondage so deep, he felt like he wouldn't ever have anymore, options. But guess what? He did. Samson was gifted by God to deliver his people, the children of Israel, from the oppression of the Philistines. As, the Spirit of God would come upon Samson, his body received superior strength and he would successfully attack the stronghold of the Philistines. Now, for example, once he was trapped inside one of their fortified cities, when they rushed to kill him. There was no way out except through the huge gate in the wall. Samson, feeling the spirit flowing through his body, he took hold of the heavy door and tore it off its hinges and carried it off on his shoulders.

Then, another time, a 1,000 soldiers of the Philistines caught him alone and swept down on the camps. Having no weapons and no one to help him, he picked up the jawbone of a dead animal and attacked. As they came at him, in waves, over and over again, he attacked repeatedly. When the battle was over Samson still stood and 1,000 soldiers of the enemy lay, dead. The word swept throughout the land, *Samson will deliver us! Samson will deliver us!* But you see, Samson was not the source of his own strength, God was. Without depending on God and obeying Him, Samson was like any other person. This came home to him and the people, when Samson grew careless, he let down his guard against Satan. He thought he could handle things by himself... *Wrong*! The Philistines, paid the most beautiful and cunning woman in their midst to discover the secret of Samson's success, Samson took his mind off of God, off his mission, and his dream. He then developed a sinful relationship with the woman, who was an enemy of the Philistines. She took him very easily, crying and pouting until she got Samson to reveal to her, the secret of his strength. Now, notice Samson's vow to God, (was symbolized by, not cutting his hair) but by allowing it to grow into, seven locks. So, as Samson lay sleeping in Delilah's arms, she was able to cut off his hair. Then, the alarm sounded inside of Samson. He then awoke, knowing his vow with God has been broken. He felt the power of God leave him and for the first time, he couldn't repel the attack of the Philistines. How awful, the Philistines took Samson and gouged out his eyes, hooked him up in place of a mule to grind at the mill of their, God, *Dagon*. Round and round, Samson went, grinding at the mill day after day, he lost his eye sight completely. His vow shattered, his *God given* strength was gone, his dreams were gone, the hopes of his people were gone. So, we must always stay focused on God's plan. Our plans don't work. Then one hot day, Samson was

Your Way is Not God's Way

grinding at the mill, sweating, hurting, bound to the mill wheel with brass fetters, out of options, when all of a sudden, he felt something on the nape of his neck. Oh, glory to God!! His hair!! It was growing, again. His head had been shaven by the Philistines, but the one thing the Philistines had not counted on, was the obvious fact that Samson's hair would grow, again. There was just a wisp of hair touching the back of his neck. Samson began to believe, again. He started feeling the Spirit of God moving in his spirit now. "*It's God!!*" he cried, "*It's God!!*" God is giving me a second chance, in that precious moment, Samson made a new decision to obey God. Samson had been careless in the way he had obeyed God. Delilah, had taken him all too easily, because he hadn't fully appreciated what God was doing in his life. The moment he felt God return, he settled it in his mind that, never again, would he disobey or fail God.

Obedience is the key to our way of life. For, when a person starts obeying God, it just causes Satan to always make mistakes. About the time the Philistines leaders 3,000 of them, were meeting in the temple of their God, celebrating their victory over Israel, by taking Samson captive, blinding him and reducing him to a beast of burden. Then, as he entered the temple packed with Lords, and Ladies of the Philistines, a big cheer goes up to their God, *Dagon*. The sightless Samson stood in the center alone.

In (Judges 16:25) it says, "And they set him between the pillars that held them up. Standing now, between the two pillars that supported the structure and the height of the entire temple." His commitment to the Lord God renewed, Samson saw a new option. With God's power, beginning to swell up inside of him, Samson asked his captors to let him feel the very pillars that were the central support for the temples, roof. I'm sure his captors, no doubt laughed and sneered, but they let Samson feel the pillars. I'm sure they shouldn't of done that either, but none the less, Samson put his arms around the two pillars and leaned his weight against them and started to, pray. The Bible records his prayer as he stood alone among the 3,000 who hated him. Wrapping his arms around the pillars and raising his sightless eyes, Samson prayed, "*Oh, Lord God remember me. Remember, me just this once, I pray thee, that I may be avenged of the Philistines for my two eyes.*"

In (Luke 18:1) it says, "Jesus said, Men ought always to pray and not to give up." There's another option good for us unless you and I pray, attacking Satan with our prayers. It's Satan. who has willed our failures and destruction. You know it's so easy to give up, to lie down and declare it's all over, and to let Satan, have his way, rather than God. It's so easy to give in, to the feeling, that you're not worth anything anymore, the enemies are right, you're no good, a failure. It's so easy to believe the Devil's lie, you have messed it all up. You don't deserve another chance. You would just throw it away like you did before. *Lies, lies, lies.* I have always said this, "I might have failed today, but I am not a failure." So very true!

Prayer still changes people, and people change things. You know, Samson could have said, "Sure, I once carried off the gates of a city and killed a thousand Philistine soldiers, with nothing but a jawbone, but how can I believe I can pull these two pillars down and bring the whole temple down with all of the enemies of the Lord God, of Israel and on myself? I've failed, the Lord and myself, so I'm out of options." Samson could've refused to attack because his options seemed so limited, so non promising, just two pillars of the temple and really what chance did he have to pull them off their foundation and cause the temples roof to collapse? Instead Samson prayed. He asked, God to remember him in spite of his failures and mistakes. Samson asked God, to grant him the Holy Spirit, to flow through his arms once more, making them like bands of steel, so he could pull the pillars down.

My good friends, God remembers you. He remembers you, even if you have failed and have let Him down again and again. I can assure you in the name of Jesus Christ of Nazareth, you can confidentally pray and call on Him anytime you are in a desperate need. God already knows your need. Use your faith, and let God take care of the problem. He's the same yesterday and today and forever and ever. Letting God handle it, trying again and seeing your dreams come true after they have seemed, shattered, forever. Through God all things are possible. Look at Samson, the crowed hooted and taunted, *Look!* Samson is struggling against those pillars. Do you suppose he's trying to pull the temples down? *Ha!*

Ha! Ha! What a fool! Can't he see how hopeless he is? Does, he think he still has strength? Of course not, Samson didn't think he had strength. For he knew he had the strength, he could feel the power of Almighty God rushing through his veins. Then as he put his arms around the pillars Samson whispered, "O Lord, remember me just this once." The Spirit of God whipped through him like a wind and flashed through him like a fire. The pillars moved under his arms. The buildings began to shake. *My God! My God!* God's strength, has come back to Samson, let's get out of here, Run, Run.

It reminds me of that old song, "He lives, He lives, Christ Jesus lives today, and He walks with me and talks to me along life's narrow ways, He lives..."

So, while 3,000 God hating Philistine, screaming spectators of their own doom. Samson locked himself with all his new found strength and pushed the pillars over off their foundations, and the roof began to collapse. The temple fell, the God, *Dagon* crushed, and the Philistines were crushed, all because of a man that had a new option. Had you or I been there and found Samson just after he had won his greatest victory, I believe we would've heard Samson saying, "My eyes have seen, the Glory of the Lord." Samson was no different from you and I, he was just a man. He had made a commitment of his life to God. You can, also see he had the Spirit of God flowing in his life. You can also see, he trusted God as his source. So, can you. My friends, God is never out of options. Our God can never be backed into a corner, that He can't get out of.

Your Way is Not God's Way

The Red Sea couldn't stop God, see Exodus chapter 14. The fiery furnace couldn't destroy Him, see-Daniel chapter 3. The prophets of Baal couldn't ruin His reputation, see-1 Kings chapter 18. Enemy kings couldn't kill Him, see-Matthew chapter 2. The grave couldn't hold Him, see-John chapter 20.

In (Philippians 4:13) we read, "I can do all things through Christ which strengtheneth me." There's a lot of glory of the Lord still waiting for you. It's not over for you, yet. There's a new beginning right now, this very hour.

Thru good times and bad times, God teaches us to give. In good times, we may have more to give, than in the bad times, but in each case, we give as a seed, we plant, that is, a seed we sow, for God to grow. The Bible, teaches this in the *Book* of Genesis. Abraham gave to God. In (Genesis 14:20) it says, "And blessed be the most high God which hath delivered thine enemies into thy hand. He gave him tithes of all." God gave back to him and his wife Sarah, a son, Isaac, when it seemed impossible. Then God, told Abraham to teach Isaac how to give in good times and bad times. When you trust God as your source as Abraham did, then good times or bad times do not affect you, as they do, to those who look, to the economy and do for themselves as their sources. You won't become proud and self centered in good times or down and out in bad times. God as your source, you can always trust Him to multiply your seeds, so you can receive back in full, your harvest. Giving and believing go together. Seeding and faith go together. So, seed is faith. You really can't have one without the other and expect to have the steady flow of God's power, miracles, and supply, coming back into your life. Our Bible teaches us these things. In (James 2:20) it says, "Faith without works is dead." In (Ephesians 2:8) it says, "Works are of no use to your eternal soul without faith." Faith and works are to go together. You're to put your faith and your seeds together. Now, your faith must be based on the Word of God, if it's going to be a steady faith. A faith that doesn't waver, but holds steady in good and bad times. Our faith must be continuous. It must endure. It must have a staying power, steadying power, and stabilizing power. How, do you get that kind of faith? In (Romans 10:17) it says, "So then faith cometh by hearing, and hearing by the Word of God." Everything, I am telling you in this book, is in the Word of God. It's coming from God, through my heart and soul, to you. As I write these words to you, you are hearing them inside of yourself and will help your faith to come. That's the way your faith is, faith is deep in your spirit. But, it's got to come up out of you and go to God in order for it to work, for you. The Word of God works in the same way with your faith. As you study the Word of God and as you hear it preached, it will cause your faith to come. It'll come up out of you and be released to God. In (Matthew 17:20) Jesus explained it like this, "Because of your unbelief, for verily I say unto you, if you can make your faith as a seed you plant, you can speak to your mountain to be removed and it will obey you. And nothing, shall be impossible to you." Our faith is like a seed, just as your giving is like a seed. A seed is ultimately what every living thing comes from. We came from the seed of our parents in conception and then, birth. Some, of our food comes from a seed planted, so does most of our clothing and items in the houses we live in, just about everything else we need and use every day. Seeds are the carriers of life. For our faith to come alive, it must work like a seed. It must grow, bear fruit, mature, and then bear even more fruit. Our faith must come up out of your spirit and grow and produce. The preaching, of the Word of God caused the seed of your faith to begin growing. I know in my heart and soul that these words, are for everyone of us. You wrap your faith around the seeds of your giving, you sew your seeds of faith in the good soil of God's work, and then and only then, do you speak to your mountain and command it, to be removed and it obeys you. Thank you, Lord! The Bible says, "that God gives seeds to the sewer." You know when I have a need, I have to give part of it away. Otherwise, I'm just stuck with my need and I don't have any hope of a seed multiplying, in God's hand. I have to give, that's the only way I can know, without any doubt and according to His Word that God, is working in my situation for me, to receive back from Him. In (Genesis 26:12) it says, "Then Isaac sowed in that land, and received in the same year a hundred fold and the Lord blessed him." Now watch this! I ask you to pay close attention, that it came back to Isaac, in the same year and in a definite time period. Listen my friends, every seed has a due season of harvest. So, therefore look for it. Every seed has multiplication power, so look for it. Our seeds don't operate on a one on one principle. Seeds will always multiply. In (Genesis 26:13) it says, "And the man (Isaac) waxed great, and went forward, and grew until he became very great." Isaac kept on planting seeds. He, also kept on believing. The Bible says, that "everywhere he went, he built an altar to the Lord." He kept God first is his life, his faith, and he kept on believing. In good times and bad times, believing, and giving the seed of faith.

Of all the things God says, about giving and receiving, one verse stands out for me and it's in the book of, (Luke 6:38) it says, "Give and it shall be given unto you, good measure, pressed down and shaken together, and running over, shall men give into your bosom. For with the same measure that ye mete withal it shall be measured to you again." Now, have you recognized that *faith* is your number one tool in attacking your needs and that you have the faith you need? Have you put your giving and your believing together? Have you started a walk of seeding and believing, of seed faith? Have you started making your giving a seed, expecting a miracle harvest, from God's treasure supply in Heaven?

Listen, never forget God wants you to win. He wants to supply your every need, and He wants you to have a fulfilled life. He wants you to have an abundant life. Overflowing with His presence, and His goodness. The Lord knows, just what you need. Thank you, Heavenly Father!

Friends, I must encourage you to make God your source today, please do it right, now. If you don't know Jesus, pray with all of your heart, first repent of the fact that your trusting in someone or something else, more than you're trusting in God. You know, that's what sin is. It's putting something, ahead of God. Decide that you are going to make God first, in your life. Accept God's Holy plan. Choose to accept Jesus as God's Son. Ask Him to enter into your being, to fill you with His Holy Spirit. Ask Him, to help you every day of your life to keep God as your source. Talk to God. Talk to Him, just like you would talk to a person, who's there in the room with you. You can say, this prayer or one like it. I feel led by the Holy Spirit to pray, *"God, I know I haven't put you first in my life, I want to. Please forgive me for all of my sins. I'm sorry I've put other things in front of you. I want to make a new, beginning. I believe that Jesus is your Son and that He is my Savior. I want to follow you, Jesus. I want to be filled with your Holy Spirit. I want to learn to do things the way you do them, to think the way you think, and to get into your kind of giving and receiving. To fill my every need in my life. The good things that are poured out to me from Heaven's treasure chests. I accept you into my heart, soul and life. Please forgive me, I pray this, right now, in the name of Jesus."* Amen and Amen. Talk to God, everyday and as often as you can. Let Him know how you feel. Tell Him you trust Him as your source.

Get into a good Bible based Church, and let God's blessings flow through your life. Be empowered in God's Word. There's power in the blessing of each of our prayers. Many times, we have to sit quietly, and be still, and listen to what God has to say to us.

Your Way is Not God's Way

Simple prayer, simple life. Let God be in everything in your life, which is done through prayer. When, a person is at their lowest, give it to the Lord, and He'll help you through it all.

When your mind, heart and soul are tuned into the Lord, He will open doors, which man has closed.

In (John 10:10) it says, "The thief cometh not, but for to steal, and to kill, and to destroy, I am come that they might have life, and that they might have it more abundantly."

In (l John 4:16) it says, "And we have known and believed the love that God hath to us. God is love and he that dwelleth in love, dwelleth in God, and God in him." You know, God's plan for our life is so much greater and better, than our own plans for our life. So, if God is for us, who would dare be against us. I once was lost, but now I am found, I was found by the grace of God. God will make a way, when there seems like there is *no way*. God is your best friend, lean on him, and pray with Him, boldly and by faith.

Chapter 5

Let me ask you a question, have you ever been sick? Why, of course we all have been sick. My dear friends, let me establish once and for all, that God wants you to be healed.

The Lord is saying, to me, "George, let my people know about my healing." In (lll John 1:2) it says, "Beloved I wish above all things that thou mayest prosper and be in health, even as thy soul prospereth."

There's another verse of Scripture, I want to share with you that can help settle the issue once and for all. In (Matthew 14:14) we read, "And Jesus went forth and saw a great multitude, and was moved with compassion toward them and He healed their sick." The only Jesus I know is a healing Jesus, the same Jesus the Bible talks about. When we read and study our Bibles, our questions about His identity, can be answered.

For there can be no mistake about who Jesus really is, if we pay close attention to what God's Word has to say about Him and God's Word indicates, that the life and ministry of Jesus was devoted to seeing people healed and made completely whole.

Now, let's take a closer look at (Matthew 14:14) in this verse lies the key to your knowing beyond any doubt that God wants to heal you, "Jesus went forth." Jesus spent some two-thirds of His time healing the sick. It seems that Jesus was always either on His way to heal someone or was in the process of healing.

This was the nature of Jesus, to heal. It's almost as if He couldn't resist. He went forth, moved and was filled with compassion to heal the sick. Once this truth saturates your mind and spirit, you'll be on your way to knowing that this same Jesus, wants to heal you, also.

There are other scriptures which can help you understand what I'm telling you. In (Exodus 15:26) it says, "I am the Lord that healeth thee." In (l Peter 2:24) it says, "By His stripes (the marks of the lashings on Jesus' back) ye are healed." In (Acts 10:38) we're told that, "God anointed, Jesus of Nazareth with the Holy Spirit and with power, who went about doing good, and healing all who were oppressed of the Devil." Because, of this scripture you and I can understand what sickness really is. Sickness is an oppression of the Devil.

Sickness isn't your friend. Furthermore, sickness isn't anybody's friend. For, sickness comes from the oppressing hand of the Devil. I know for sure there are some people who are confused about this matter and believe that sickness comes from God, that God is trying to punish them. But just think about what this would mean. If, God puts sickness on people, then why did he send Jesus to heal? Wouldn't God and Jesus be working against each other, when Jesus Himself said, in (John 5:19) "The Son can do nothing of Himself, but what he seeth the Father do, for what things soever He doeth, these also doeth, these also doeth the Son likewise." So my dear friends, there's absolutely no reason for you and me to be deceived about this matter.

In (John 10:10) Jesus said, "The thief (the Devil) cometh not but to steal and to kill, and to destroy." That's what the Devil's about. His whole nature and purpose is to wreck your life. He wants to destroy you. He wants to take away your Salvation. He also, wants to steal your health, your family, and your finances and also, destroy your emotions. But you see, Jesus also said, in the second part of (John 10:10) "I have come that they might have life, and they might have it more abundantly." Jesus didn't come that you might be sick. He, came that you might have life and have it more abundantly.

You know, I'd love to sum it up this way. Jesus came:

1-To take off you, what the Devil put on you.
2-To take out of you, what the Devil put in you.
3-To put back on you, what the Devil took off of you.
4-To put back in you, what the Devil took out of you.

So you see, I think we've had enough of the negative type of thinking, where we wrongfully, blame

God for our sickness, when He's really the one who wants to heal us. Please don't think for a moment that God caused you to be sick. That's the Devil's business through and through. God wants to heal you. God's not going to get any Glory out of your sickness or affliction. Sickness is the Devils oppression.

Here are the words I would say, to you right now. "Lets, now begin to know, God wants to heal you, by accepting the fact that it's His nature to heal. Healing is the nature of Jesus. Jesus went forth and healed."

Of course, when Jesus looked at the crowd which followed Him, He saw more than just a great multitude of people. Jesus doesn't look at a crowd in the same way you or I would. Jesus sees them as individuals. And He sees, that everyone is sick in some way, spiritually, physically, emotionally, financially or in broken homes or family relationships.

Jesus sees only you, as an individual, also. He knows who you are. Jesus knows, your name and also knows where you live. He knows, the very count of hairs on your head. He knows, what you are going through, right now, at this very moment of your life.

I can sense in my spirit when something is wrong. I'm beginning to understand that we are all sick in some way or another, and we'll need God's healing power to touch some or all areas of our lives. To Him, you're unique and irreplaceable. You're unique in that there's only one of, you. You're irreplaceable and nobody can take your place. *I mean nobody*!

Listen, your life is God's gift to you, and what you make of your life is your gift back to Him. Jesus, sees the potential in your life, and He also sees that the Devil would just love to steal your potential away through, sickness.

To the Devil, you're another nameless soul. But to Jesus, you are the crowning masterpiece of God's creation and he'll go to uttermost bounds to see you saved and healed when you yield your life to Him.

This is what happened when Jesus went forth and saw the multitude. This is what happens when Jesus looks at us today, His power is unlimited. Except by, our faith and willingness, to receive Him. Oh yes, He wants to heal you. The question is, will you accept His healing power, not just as something to read about in the Bible? It's something to be received, on a very personal and individual level.

For, He was moved with compassion toward them. When you're confronted with someone who is sick, one of two things will usually happen. You'll either be moved toward the sick person, or you'll be drawn away. Jesus was moved with compassion, towards the multitudes, where as sympathy allows a person to stand idly by and say, "I'm so sorry," now compassion demands that you do something. Compassion fills you with an irresistible urge to reach out to the sick person, to do something, by releasing your faith, to help get rid of what's wrong. For, it's Christ in you identifying with the person in need. This kind of compassion, goes hand in hand, with the way Jesus looks upon the individual. What He sees, creates the desire to do something. The compassion He feels, locks in with His force and moves Him into action. As, you begin to understand what compassion is all about you'ill discover, it's the missing link in your own life, knowing that God wants to heal you.

Even when everything else seems right, it still takes divine compassion, for you to have a point of contact to receive your miracle from the Lord. Now, this is what compassion is all about. When you believe and receive by faith, the understanding, that Jesus, has compassion towards you, right now, no matter where you are this can be the moment for a healing miracle to begin. This is the real Jesus. This is the healing Jesus, doing what He was called to do, and being what He, was called to be. This is the real Jesus saying, in (Luke 4:18) "The Spirit of the Lord is upon me, because He has anointed me to preach the Gospel to the poor, He hath sent me to heal the brokenhearted, to preach deliverance to the captives, and recovering of sight to the blind, to set at liberty them that are bruised." Above everything else.

Please, I want you to know this real Jesus in a personal way, on an intimate level. For He, gave His life for your Salvation. His body was lashed and beaten that you might be healed. Let the issue be settled. And, let it be established in your heart, mind, and soul, today. God wants to heal you. Right now, I just feel the compassion of Jesus. So, I want to pray for you right now. *"Heavenly Father, I come to you in the name of Jesus, whose life and ministry brings us all your healing power to all who are sick and oppressed by the Devil. I pray, dear Lord that we'll feel your healing power, this very moment. And, dear friends and loved ones, I pray that through this message from God's Word, your faith will be released and you'll know God wants to heal you. Oh yes, from the crown of your head to the soles of your feet, may you begin to receive your healing, right now. In Jesus' name we pray. Amen and Amen.* I always feel so much better after praying. Thank you, Jesus.

With, healing I must tell you about what happened to me, back in 1985. I had five blood clots in my brain. Three was in front of my brain, and two were in the back of my brain. Blood clots float around in your body, and then they become lodged in very narrow openings. The two blood clots in the back of my brain where the clots lodged, affected my breathings. I worked in a hot uniform factory. It was lunch time, so I went outside for lunch. I must say, "three days before this all happened, I had a migraine headache, every time I would bend, over my head would pound harder." I thought it was just a headache,and it would just go away. Well, that never happened.

On the day I went outside for lunch the last thing I remembered was getting ready to eat my lunch. Well, that never happened. I came in too, in the middle of the parking lot, with my lunch still there. I had bitten a big chunk of my tongue off, my head still hurting, my eyes felt like they were going to burn right out of their sockets.

I had no idea, as to what had happened to me. I was in a dazed condition. What had happened, was I had a "grandma seizer." I had never had one of those ever in my life. I knew something was wrong, but I didn't know what. Thank God for animals. My oldest sister Sylvia, called me one day, concerned about a baby kitten she had found in her yard, she lived in the country. It was near death, and my sister wanted to know if I wanted the kitten and of course, myself being an animal lover, assured her that I would take the kitten. The kitten was so close to death, that I named her Wonder, (*Because it was a wonder she was still alive*) I loved this cat, nursed her back to health. She had two litters of kittens. I had her for eighteen years.

When I had this grandma seizer in the parking lot, I knew something was wrong, but the only thing I could think of was getting home and feeding and watering my cat, Wonder. I lived four miles from where I worked. I walked all the way home, don't know how I managed to do that. I got home, took care of Wonder, told her "that something was wrong with me, I didn't know what, but I had to get to the hospital and get it checked out."

Then, I walk to the hospital, by the time I got there, I wasn't fully aware of what was going on. At the hospital they took C.A.T. scans of my brain. Come to find out, I had five blood clots in my brain. The three in the front of my brain, they gave me blood thinner to dissolve them, the clots in the back of my brain they had to do emergency surgery. Where the clots lodged, affected my breathing. It was a life and death surgery. My doctor was a very sweet *lady,* surgeon. She told me when the surgery was all completed, "if I would have waited five more minutes, I would of went into a coma and died." But, you see the Lord wasn't ready for me yet.

While I was in surgery, (and still under) I had a vision, that I went to Heaven. My soul went up to meet Jesus. I seen the river of life. It was like gold sand, swirling in a big circle. In the middle was the most beautiful light, the most clear colors I have ever seen, it was just beautiful. On the inside was a big cross with Jesus standing behind it holding out His hands toward me. I felt no pain, I was completely calm, I was not afraid. As I got closer to Him, I was as close to Him as a hand shake. He spoke to me and said, "George, I am not finished with you yet. Look up and when you see the light, then you will know what I want from you." I humbly asked the Lord, "just what was it, that He wanted me to do for Him? What was His plan? To this day, I still don't know exactly what He wants me to do. But, I will always do what Jesus wants me to do. Wow, what a peace we have with God. The Lord picked me, for He knew that I would do it for Him. He knows all things, *All Things*. After the surgery, I opened my eyes, I thought my doctor was an Angel, she was wearing all white. She kept saying, "George! George! I just smiled at her and I asked her, "if she believed in visions." She said, "Yes George." She was so happy that I had made it through the surgery and so was I. You know that was back in 1985, and I remember this as clearly today, as I did then. No, matter what condition, physically you're in, our Heavenly Father is there to heal you completely. He is always there by our side, ready to heal us when we need it. For it was real, just like our Heavenly Father is.

In (John 14:2) it says, "In my father's house are many mansions, if it were not so, I would of told you. I go to prepare a place for you." In (Exodus 15:2) it says, "The Lord is my strength and song, and He is become my Salvation." In (Jeremiah 6:16) it says, "Stand ye in the ways and see, where is the good way, and walk theirin and ye shall find rest for your souls." In (Psalms 23:4) it says, "Yea, though I walk through the valley of the shadow of death, I will fear no evil, for thou art with me, thy rod and thy staff they comfort me." In (Deuteronomy 7:9) it says, "The Lord thy God, He is God, the faithful God, which keepeth covenant and mercy with them that love Him."

So, years after my surgery, I continued to have, *grandma seizers*. There were no pre-warnings, when, I would have them. Years later, the Lord healed me of those awful seizers. They were very dangerous, a person could have a stroke, go into a coma and die.

I must tell you more about myself. I've been through pure hell and back many times. But the Lord, helped me through each and every time. I'm not proud of my mistakes, but I did learn from them.

In my younger days, when I left home when I was 18 years old. I got into drugs, became a drug dealer, I had D.U.I. convictions, sold guns, been to prison. I was on my way, straight to hell. But, just like Daniel and the lions den, while I was in prison, that's where I found the Lord.

In (Isaiah 41:10) it says, "Fear not for I am with thee, be not dismayed, for I am thy God I will strengthen thee, yea I will help thee." That's where, in prison, our God healed me of the "grandma seizers."

Your Way is Not God's Way

Sometimes, the Lord will take you out of where you are and put you somewhere where He can work with you. I know this on a personal level, for the Lord did it for me. No matter what you have done, or have been through, our Lord will forgive you, He loves you and will keep you.

Chapter 6

You know, living in the natural world, it's easy to get the idea that people are your source of supply. This is also, where you can miss the truth of God's Holy Word. God often uses people, as the means of our supply, but God Himself is the source. People are merely instruments. By looking to God as your only source, you can be confident, positive, and expectant that He can provide everything you need. I have been living God's way now, for many years. I belong to the biggest gang in the world and that's, "God's gang."

That's why I named this book, "**<u>Your</u> <u>Way</u> <u>is</u> <u>Not</u> <u>God's</u> <u>Way</u>**." My way, didn't work, but God's way is the only way. In (Matthew 5:8) it says, "Blessed are the pure in heart for they shall see God." In (Psalms 121:8) it says, "The Lord shall preserve thy going out and thy coming in from this time forward, and even forever more." In (Luke 11:9) Jesus says, and I say unto you "Ask and it shall be given to you, seek, and ye shall find, knock, and it shall be opened unto you." This makes us look forward to every new day, as the most important day in our life. Why? Because you know God, is your source.

Like Jesus, giving is becoming your lifestyle. Therefore, you can expect a miracle, in the form of the answer to your need, everyday. This will create a joy and an opportunity in your new way of life.

In (ll Corinthians 5:17) it says, "Therefore if any man be in Christ, he is a new creature, old things are passed away, behold, all things are become new."

If you have never accepted Jesus Christ into your heart, I encourage you to do so right, now. Just pray this simple prayer out loud with me. *"Lord, I want to make you the source of my life. I come before you with a humble heart and confess that I have never made you the top priority in my life. I've sinned, Lord. I've missed the mark with my life. Please forgive me. I believe you died on the cross and rose again, and because you did, I can have eternal life with you. Come into my heart, Lord Jesus, and be my personal Lord and Savior. I make you the source of my life and ask you to show me how I can best serve you. In Jesus' precious name we pray."* Amen and Amen.

In (Mark 8:35) it says, "Whosoever will save his life shall lose it, but whosoever shall lose his life for my sake and the Gospels, the same shall save it." Thank you, Lord. In (ll Corinthians 5:10) it says, "For we must all appear before the judgment seat of Christ, that every one may receive the things done in his body, according to that he hath done, whether it be good or bad."

Let's love one another as never before. Let's win souls to Christ as never before. Let's keep ourselves unspotted, from the world as never before. Let's love and obey. Jesus faithfully remembering that our allegiance is to Him.

You know, we all can remember, when time seemed to go by slowly and also, when it flew by. The older a person gets, the days seem to grow shorter. Then for some, time ends and eternity begins. Time ends, but eternity lasts forever. We're all only one heartbeat from eternity. Where will we be when our time runs out? Dropping off the edge of time, to a place we rather not be? Or, will we be called away to a lovely place, where God has prepared for us? What we find time for here on earth, determines our own eternity. Time is a gift from God. Let's use it well.

In (l Peter 1:25) it says, "The Word of the Lord endureth forever and this is the Word which by the Gospel is preached unto you." Learn to receive from God, from people who want to bless you, and from yourself. For God, is a God of purpose. No matter what happens in our life, if we'll keep praying and trusting God, keep loving Him and walking in His will, to the best of our ability. He'll cause everything, to work out for the good. Whatever, happened to us in the past, may not have been good in itself. And, it may have led to a struggle with acceptance and desire for approval, but because God is good, He can take a different and painful thing and cause it to work out for our good and the good of others.

We, may not always understand His purpose, but we can be sure, He definitely has one. Something that may look terrible to us, and yet all the while God, intends to show His glory, by working something good from it.

We often wonder sometimes, why God waits so long to come to our rescue or why He allows certain things to take place. We can't always figure out what God is doing, or even why, He is doing it, but if we trust Him, He will make something wonderful from it. You must know who you are in Jesus.

Understand that your righteousness is found only in Christ. All you have to do is receive by faith, what Jesus has already provided. Let faith, take the lead and your feelings, will follow.

You must believe that God loves you. Affirm it to yourself daily, through meditating on it and speaking it. Start believing you have been excepted by Jesus. Ask Him, for favor with the right people, and don't worry about all the others who seem valuable to you.

This is very important. See yourself, as complete in Christ. You'll be encouraged to press toward what you already know is yours. Jesus desires that you feel whole, complete and satisfied. It's God's will, and therefore, spiritual and pleasing to Him to see ourselves in Christ. We should believe, that if we have repented of our sins and accepted Jesus as our Savior, He has given us His righteousness. We're to walk in this life, with our heads held high, because we are children of God and He loves us. Thank you, Lord!

You know, sometimes the only way we can find out what we're meant to be doing in life, is to step out and try some new things. God promises to forgive our

Your Way is Not God's Way

past mistakes. Failure is part of every real success, because failing our way to success humbles us. You will succeed, if you refuse to stop trying, because prayer released power into our lives. For, if you have God, you have all you need. The most vital things for any Christian are prompt, hearty obedience to God.

God, expects a person to put, *Him first*, then his family, then his home, and his health. If a person loses their job, as in my case, then God will help you get a better job. I've always believed this, pray often, use wisdom, and be patient, and wait on the Lord.

We may not always understand, but we can trust in God, to supply our every need. It reminds me, one Sunday morning I was watching my Christian channel on T.V. and Jerry Farewell was preaching. At the very end of his program, he had a 2 year course, that he was offering. The course covered the whole entire Bible. A person could go to Lynchburg, V.A. to the college for 2 years for $24,000.00 or you could take the course through the *Liberty Home Bible Institute*. I would have to put down $250.00 then, pay $42.00 a month for 24 months. Well, I knew I couldn't go to Lynchburg, V.A. College for 2 years. The Lord was speaking to my heart concerning this. I prayed over this matter, "Lord, if this is your will, let your will be done." I went and told my wife Cathy, about what the Lord had put on my heart. I told her the 2 options, that he had available for the course. Cathy said, "If it's the Lord's will, honey I'm behind you 100 %." Well, I prayed some more about it. The Lord just kept on telling me to call and get the ball rolling. So, that following Sunday I watched the show, again. The Lord again, said "to make the call." I didn't waste a second. I called the number and got it set up, I was never so sure about anything, like this in my life. This is how good our Lord works. This was a 2 year course, I completed the whole course in 1 year. I started in 02-02-06 and finished 01-05-07 and I went to my graduation in Lynchburg V.A. on 05-19-07 at 9:30 A.M.

Like I've said, "if God's in your plans, and it's God's will, He will supply whatever your need is." And you know what? I was a straight A student, on the twenty-second final exam. I scored seven 100's. God's way is the only way to go. I know God has a lot more for me to do, for His will and His work here on this earth.

God loves us, and that's all I need to know. He died for us, our sins, and He's in Heaven preparing a place for you and me.

My goal is to get as many people, through God's will, to except God's plan of Salvation, so we can meet on those streets of gold with our Lord. I'm going to explain, the plan of Salvation more in the following pages.

Let's start with, what kind of path are you on? We're on the path of life. I got on the path of life, when I was born. You got on the path of life, when you were born. You and I are walking together on the path of life. The best way to help us as we go along is the Bible. There's no other book like it, because the Bible, is the Word of God. There are two roads ahead of us. One is a narrow road and leading up. The other is a broad road leading down. In life, we must choose

Your Way is Not God's Way

one of these roads. No one, else can make the choice for us. Therefore, we must choose for ourselves, which road we are going to take in this life.

Our Lord, Jesus Christ told us where these roads lead. The broad roads lead to total destruction. Many people are on this busy road. The narrow road leads to everlasting life in, Heaven. You ask, "What is Heaven?" Heaven, is God's home and it's more beautiful than anything we could ever imagine. The Bible tells us, about the city of God. It's made of pure gold, with all kinds of precious stones.

There is no need of the sun or moon in Heaven, because, the glory of God lights up Heaven. There are no nights there. Everything in Heaven is clean and pure, no sin or impure thing, will ever be allowed to enter this city in Heaven. There's no sorrow, crying, pain and no death. All our loved ones, who died trusting Jesus, will be there, we'll know our loved ones and they'll know us. Oh, what a reunion that will be. Best of all, we'll see our Lord and Savior. That's where I want to go, and I am sure you want to, also. Now, here's some wonderful news for you. God wants you to be in Heaven with Him.

Do you know, why God wants you to be in Heaven? I'll tell you, because He loves you and me. It doesn't matter who you are, what you look like, or where you live, God loves you. And, He wants you to be in Heaven with Him.

Now, here's something we must do if we want to go to Heaven. We must choose the narrow road, by taking the Lord Jesus as our Savior. No one can do this for you. Let's see, there are 5 steps on this

Your Way is Not God's Way

narrow road that leads to Heaven. Each step have words on them. On:

Step 1-I have sinned.
Step 2-God loves me.
Step 3-Christ died for me.
Step 4-I receive Him.
Step 5-I have everlasting life-then Heaven.

Now, I'm going to explain each step, and with each step, I will have a Bible verse for each step. I want to keep these steps, as simple as I can.

Step 1-I have sinned. In (Romans 3:23) it says, "For all have sinned, and come short of the glory of God." This means, that we have all said and done wrong things. In His Word, God tells us what is right and what is wrong. But, we all have broken God's commandments. We have all sinned. Have you ever told a lie, stolen anything, disobeyed your parents, ever said curse words, or used God's name in a vein, or ever hated someone?

God says, that these things are sins and we can't go to Heaven with sins in our hearts. Sin is a terrible thing. It hurts us and hurts others. The worst thing about sin, is it hurts God's heart, too. It's because He loves us. Is God speaking to your heart right now, and reminding you of some wrong things that you have said or done? If you want to be saved, you must be sorry for your sins and want to stop doing them.

Step 2-God loves me. In (John 3:16) it says, "For God so loved the world, that He gave his only begotten Son, that whosoever believeth in Him should not perish, but have everlasting life." Because we are sinners, we need a Savior. This verse, tells us that God has given His Son, to us to be our Savior. This means, that He gave the Lord Jesus, to die on the cross for our sins. When God says, "the world." He means everyone in this old world. That includes you and me! When He says, "whosoever." He means everyone.

Step 3-Christ died for me. In (Romans 5:8) it says, "God commandeth (God showed) His loves toward us, in that, while we were yet sinners, Christ died for us." This verse tells us that God loved us while we were yet sinners and that He gave His Son to die for us. You know, God couldn't overlook our sins or pretend that He didn't know about them. God must punish sin. God allowed the Lord Jesus to take our punishment. He allowed Jesus to die for our sins. The Lord Jesus died for sinners. He died for you and He died for me. Go ahead and say it, "Christ died for me." Not only did Christ die for our sins, but He also rose again from the dead. He's our living Savior! He has all power in Heaven and in this earth. He can forgive your sins and make you a child of God.

Step 4-I receive Him. The next verse tells us how to become a child of God. In (John 1:12) it says, "As many as received Him, (the Lord Jesus Christ) to them gave he power to become the sons of God, even to them that believe on His name." To become a child of God, you must come as a sinner, to the Lord Jesus and receive Him as your Savior. God has given the Lord Jesus to you to be your Savior, but you must receive Him, you must take Him as your own Savior.

When you take the Lord Jesus, as your Savior you become a child of God. You ask,"How do I take the Lord Jesus as my Savior?" You do so, by asking Him to come into your heart. Your heart is like a house, with a door. Jesus said, in (Revelation 3:20) "Behold I stand at the door, and knock, if any man hear my voice, and opens the door, I will come in to him, and will sup with him, and he with me."

Step 5-I have everlasting life. In (John 3:36), it says, "He that believes on the Son has everlasting life, and he that believeth not the Son shall not see life, but the wrath of God abideth on Him." This verse tells us that, if we believe on the Lord Jesus, we have everlasting life. I hope you understand, what I have been writing.

Now are you ready to make your choice? Would you like to choose the road that leads straight to Heaven? You can take Christ, as your Savior right here and right now. You will always be glad in your heart that you did. Listen, since this is just between you and the Lord, it would be best, if you find a quiet place, where you can be a alone for a few minutes or so. This is the most important thing you'll ever do in your life. So, right now, before you read my next part, go ahead, find a quiet place where you can be alone with the Lord Jesus. Think carefully about each step and say the words softly to yourself and the Lord Jesus:

> 1-I have sinned. Lord Jesus I know that I have sinned and I am truly sorry for my sins.

2-God loves me. Father, I thank you for loving me, so much and for giving your Son to die for my sins.

3-Christ died for me. Lord Jesus I do believe that you are the Son of God and that you died on the cross for my sins. Thank you, for loving me so, much.

4-I receive Him. Lord Jesus, please come into my heart and be my Savior. Right now, I take you as my Savior. Please forgive me of my sins and make me a child of God.

5-I have everlasting life. Thank you, Lord Jesus for coming into my heart and for being my Savior and thank you for giving me everlasting life. When I believe that Jesus died for my sins, and I receive Him as my savior, I have everlasting life. I'm saved, my sins are forgiven. I'm a child of God. It's just as simple as that.

How do we know we have everlasting life? We know because God says so in His Word. The Bible says, in (John 3:36) "He that believes on the Son has everlasting life." Whose word is this? It's God's Word. So, we know that it is true. God said it! I believe it! And you know what, that settles it!

Being a child of God is the most wonderful thing in this entire world, but let me let you in on a little secret. It will not always be easy while we are here in this earth. We'll have many troubles and trails as we travel to our wonderful home in Heaven. But, we don't have to be afraid of the Lord Jesus. He's living in our hearts, he has promised in (Hebrews 13:5) "I will never leave you." I'm saved, thank you, Lord. Being saved is the most precious truth in the entire Bible. Remember, being saved, is the most important thing in the entire world. **God loves you!**

Chapter 7

Now, you might be asking, "What is God like?" We all need to know about God because we all need Him. The Lord Jesus said, in (John 17:3), "This is life eternal, that they might know thee the only true God, and Jesus Christ, whom thou hast sent." God's so great and so wonderful that we can never know all there's to know about Him. But, God has told us many things about Himself in the Bible. From the Bible we learn that there's only one God, yet He is in three persons, Father, Son and Holy Spirit. The *Father* is God, the *Son* is God and the *Holy Spirit* is God. Now, God the Father is in Heaven. God the Son, is the Lord Jesus Christ, who came into this world to be our Savior. God the Holy Spirit dwells in the hearts, of all who have received the Lord Jesus as their Savior.

The Bible, tells us many other things that are true about God. In (Genesis 1:1) it says, "In the beginning, God created the Heaven and the earth." God is the creator. Have you ever wondered how the earth, sun moon and the stars came into being? God created them! This universe didn't come into being by itself. God created it! Now, we know that there is a God, because we can see what He has done.

We see the wonderful things which He has created. The Bible says, in (Psalms 19:1) "The Heavens declare the Glory of God, and the firmament sheweth His handywork." God created us, also. We are very special creatures, because we were created in the image of God. The Bible says, in (Genesis 1:27) "So, God created man in His own image, in the image of God created he Him, male and female created he them."

Do you know what God loves the most? God loves people. He's so great that He knows each one of us. He knows and loves you. You're worth more to Him than the world. For God is eternal. This means that God has always been. God has no beginning and He will have no end. Everything else in the universe had a beginning, but there never was a time, when God didn't exist. The Bible says, in (Psalms 90:2) "Before the mountains were brought forth, or ever thou hadst formed the earth and the world, even from everlasting to everlasting, thou art God." So, therefore, God is everywhere. Which means that God's presents is everywhere in His universe. Our God is great!

In (Jeremiah 23:24) it says, "Can any hide himself in secret places that I shall not see him? Saith the Lord. Do not I fill Heaven and earth? Saith the Lord." No matter, where we're at, or where we may go, God is there. I know perhaps you are wondering, if God everywhere, why can't we all, see Him? It's a very good question. Now, the reason we can't see God is because God is a Spirit. And we can't see a Spirit, right? We all have a body which we all can see. But, you also have a Spirit which we can't see. We see our bodies, but no one can see our Spirit. God is all Spirit, and He doesn't have a body, so we can't see Him. But, He sees us, He hears us, and He loves us. Because God *is* God and because He's a Spirit, He can, be everywhere at the same time. He's always with us wherever we are. So God, is *almighty*, which means that God can do anything. There's no limit to His power. He's the almighty God, He has all power in Heaven and this earth. You know, even the most powerful men in this world, are as nothing, compared to our God. In (Daniel 4:35) it says, "And all the inhabitants of the earth are reputed as nothing: he doeth according to His will in the army of Heaven, and among the inhabitants of the earth, and none can stay His hand, or say unto Him, what doest thou?"

Our God is all wise, this means that God knows all things. For, He knows everything that has happened, and He knows everything that's going to happen. God knows the number of stars in the sky. He also calls them by name.

In (Genesis 16:13) it says, "And she called the name of the Lord that spake unto her, thou God seest me. For she said, have I also here looked after Him that seeth me" God knows, all that we have said and have done. He knows what we think. He knows every secret we have. He sees us *At All* times. Our God, is *Holy,* which means God is without any sin. God is all light and glory. Therefore, because God is Holy, he hates sin, and loves righteousness. In the Bible darkness is sin. In (l John 1:5) it says, "This then the message which we have heard of Him, and declare unto you, that God is light, and in Him is no darkness at all."

The Bible says, of God, "God is light, and in Him is no darkness at all." God once spoke to the prophet Isaiah in a vision. A vision is something like a dream. In his vision, Isaiah saw God upon His throne. Around the throne of God, Angles were praising God. In the Bible they were saying, in (Isaiah 6:3) it says, "Holy, Holy, Holy is the Lord of the hosts, the whole earth is full of His glory." When Isaiah saw the vision, he was afraid. The vision showed him that God is Holy and for he knew that he was sinful. He fell on his face and cried.

In (Isaiah 6:5) he said, "Woe is me! For I am undone, because I am a man of unclean lips, and I dwell in the midst of a people of unclean lips, for mine eyes have the King, the Lord of host." We also are sinful, yet our God wants us to come to Him. He has made a way so that we can come into His presence. When we take the Lord Jesus as our Savior, God sees us in Christ. God says, "that we are clean and pure in his sight because we are "in Christ". Our God is just, meaning that God always does what is right. He's Holy and just, therefore God must punish sin. He can't overlook our sins or pretend that He doesn't know about them,

When we turn from our sins and take Christ as our Savior. God is faithful and just to forgive us of our sins. Christ paid for our sins by His death on the cross. The Bible says, in (l John 2:12) "I write unto you, little children, because your sins are forgiven you for His name's sake." God is love. God loves us and wants only what is best for us. God showed his great love for us, by sending His Son, the Lord Jesus, to die on the cross for our sins.

In (Romans 5:8) it says, "But God commandeth (God showed) His love toward us, in that, while we were yet sinners, Christ died for us." Even though we may not know why, troubles, sickness, and trials happen to us. God wants us to trust Him. Even, when we are sick or whatever may come our way, we must believe, that God loves us and He does what is best for us. God is faithful and He always keeps His word. Sometimes we forget. Sometimes we make promises, that we can't keep. God never forgets. God, *Always* keeps His promises.

In (Hebrews 10:23) it says, "Let us hold fast profession of our faith without wavering, (For He is faithful that promised)." God is unchangeable, He's always the same in His Holy nature and His character. God's always Holy, righteous, just, and loving. God said, of Himself, in (Malachi 3:6) "For I am the Lord, I change not, therefore ye sons of Jacob are not consumed." Here's some amazing truth, did you know that God once was a man? Yes, the Son of God once came into the world as a little baby. In (Isaiah 9:6) it says, "For unto us a Child is born, unto us a Son is given, and the goverment shall be upon His shoulders, and His name shall be called Wonderful Counsellor,The mighty God, the everlasting Father, the Prince of Peace." He came into this world as a little baby, born in a stable, yet He is "The mighty God." The Lord Jesus was a man, yet He is God.

In (1 Timothy 3:16) it says, "And without controversy great is the mystery of godliness, God was manifest in the flesh, justified in the Spirit, seening of angles, preached unto the Gentiles, believed on in the world, received up into Glory." Now, here's a very important question, why did the Lord Jesus come into the world? Okay, we are sinners; he came because you and I needed a Savior. We have said and done some wrong things. God is Holy and just, therefore, He must punish sin. He's love, He gave His son to die in our place. The precious truth in the Bible, is that the Son of God loved us so much that He left Heaven and became a man so that He could die for our sins. The Lord Jesus has died on the cross, God forgives the sins of all those who take Christ as their Savior. Our God doesn't over look our sins, but He forgives them, because He sees the blood of His son which was shed for them.

In (Colossians 1:14) it says, "In whom we have redemption through His blood, even the forgiveness of sins." Have you trusted the Lord Jesus as your Savior? If you have, then all your sins have been forgiven. You're a child of God. God is your Heavenly Father, and you can always depend on Him for all your everyday needs. What a wonderful blessing this is for us. After reading about just how great God is and how much He loves us, what does it make you want to do? Why, of course it makes you want to worship Him and praise Him. And that's exactly what God wants you to do. So, right now, find your quiet place where you can talk to God in prayer. Tell Him how great and wonderful you think He is. If there's sin in your life, confess that sin to God. Thank Him, for sending the Lord Jesus to die for your sins. Thank Him for serving you. Praise Him for His greatness and His goodness.

In (Psalms 145:3) it says, "Great is the Lord, and greatly to be praised, and His greatness is unsearchable." God's so great, that He not only created the universe, but He also knows and loves us. Thank you, Lord.

Chapter 8

It's so wonderful to be a Christian, but we must realize that the road to Heaven will not be so easy. Why? Because, we have many enemies. The Bible tells us about three enemies against, us Christians.

   1-World.
   2-Flesh.
   3-The Devil.

They try to get us to sin. But God has made a way for us to have victory over them.

1-*The world.* Now, God wants us to love Him with all of our hearts. Satan, doesn't want us to love God, so he uses the attractive things of this world, to draw us away from loving God and wanting to do His will. Some of these things may not be sinful, by themselves, but if they take first place in our life, that's when, they become sinful for us. If they cause us to spend less time in prayer and reading God's Word or keeps us away from Church on the Lord's Day, they're sinful for us.

The Bible says, in (1 John 2:15) "Love not the world, neither the things that are in the world. If any man love the world, the love of the Father is not in him." The Bible says, "Christ gave Himself for our sins that He might deliver us from our present evil world." God wants us to overcome the world and it's sinful attractions. Now, the question arises. How can we overcome the world? We, do so by loving the Lord Jesus, with all of our hearts. This world has many attractive things and sinful pleasures,but they don't really satisfy our hearts. Only Christ can do this.

Do you want to have more love for Christ? Think of His great love for you and how He suffered and died for your sins, you will love Him more and more. If you truly love the Lord Jesus, you will love the things of God, and not things of the world. In (Colossians 3:2) it says, "Set your affection on things above, not on things on the earth."

2-Now, this is a big one here, *the Flesh*. What is "the flesh?" The flesh is our sinful, human nature. Another name for it is *Self*. Self is what we are inside. Now, to find out what we are really like inside, let's see what self is like. *Self* is very proud. In fact, self thinks that he/she is the most important person in the world. Self wants everyone to look up to him/her. Self is completely selfish. He/she lives to please him/her self. Self, always wants to have his/her own way, and he/she hates to have to obey someone else. *Self* never likes to admit that he/she is wrong. He/she always tries to blame someone else. *Self* is easily offended or hurt. *Self* doesn't like to forgive others, instead *Self*

Your Way is Not God's Way

holds grudges. God tells us, that we should forgive others, but *Self* never wants to obey God. You know, we may not like to admit it, but this is the way we are, on the inside. *Self* has been on the throne of our hearts. When we were saved, another person came to live in our heart, and that's the Lord Jesus Christ. So wonderful, but there's still a problem. The problem is, that *Self* didn't move out! *Self* is still in our heart. Perhaps you have already noticed that, you still do things that you shouldn't do. For that reason, *Self* is still on the throne of your heart. When *Self* is on the throne, we commit many sins. We are proud, selfish, disobedient, we quarrel, lose our tempers, and are unforgiving. These sins hurt the heart of the Lord Jesus. They make Him ashamed of us. God wants us to have complete victory over *Self*. So, you're asking, what's the secret of victory over *Self*? The real secret is to make Christ the King of your life. We must take self off the throne and put Christ, there. The Lord Jesus, really does have the right to be King in our life. Why? Because we belong to Him. For the Bible, tells us so, in (l Corinthians 6:19-20) "Know ye not that your body is the temple of the Holy Ghost which is in you, which ye have of God, and ye are not your own. For ye are bought with a price, therefore glorify God in your body, and in your spirit, which are God's." What was the price the Lord Jesus paid for us? The price was His own blood. He gave His life to redeem us. We belong to Christ. He has every right to be King in our heart. Even though, Christ has the right to be our King, He waits for us, to tell Him, that we want Him to rule as the King in our life.

When Christ is on the throne in our heart, we'll have His love, joy, peace in our hearts. We *will not* commit the sins of, *Self.* You must make a choice between *Self* and *Christ*. You must decide who is going to be on the throne of your heart. If you, choose to make Christ the King of your life, that means, you must obey Him. I know, you want Christ to be your King, don't you? Let's, stop right now and tell Him that you really want Him to be your King. Here's a prayer that you can pray with me, *"Heavenly Father, Lord Jesus, we thank you for loving us so much and for dying for us. We belong to you, and now we want you to be on the throne in our hearts, and to be the King in our life. We want to obey you and do your will. In the name of Jesus we pray." Thank you, Lord! Amen and Amen.* Now, remember if Christ is your King, you must live to please Him and not, *Self.*

3-Here's the worst and greatest enemy of us Christians, it's *the Devil*, and he's also called, Satan. The Bible says, in (l Peter 5:8) "Be sober, be vigilant, because your adversary the Devil, as a roaring lion, walketh about, seeking whom he may devour." When you take Christ as your Savior, you took a step that made Satan very angry. You, left him and joined those who trust in the Lord Jesus, for Satan, knows that he can't keep you from going to Heaven, but nonetheless, he will still do all he can, to tempt you and get you to sin.

How does the Devil tempt us? For him, it's very easy, he does so by putting wrong thoughts into our minds. Satan can do this himself or he can use things such as movies, TV, or dirty books etc. to put wrong thoughts into our minds. For Satan, it's whatever it takes, to make you sin, he'll do it. Satan will tempt you with immorality and use sex to cause you to, sin. He'll tempt you to use drugs or to drink. It, just doesn't matter to Satan. For, he knows that these things will destroy your body and mind. Even when you sin, Satan will try to make you think, that God is angry with you and that he won't forgive you. Satan will try to discourage you and make you fearful and afraid. Satan is the worst and most terrible enemy.

The question is, "can we defeat Satan by ourselves?" No, we can't. He's much too powerful for us. But, here's the great news, Christ has already defeated Satan for us. When Christ died on the cross, Satan thought he had won a great victory. But Christ didn't stay in the grave, He rose from the dead. Our Lord Jesus Christ was victorious over Satan and all the powers of darkness. Christ won against Satan. Yes, since Christ is our Savior and we belong to Him, we share in His victory over Satan. Christ's victory is OUR victory.

The Lord Jesus, has set us free from Satan's power. We don't have to be afraid, of Satan. Why? You ask, because Christ lives in us and He is greater and stronger than Satan.

The Bible says, in (l John 4:4) "Ye are of God, little children, and have overcome them, because greater is He that is in you, than he that is in the world." This means, that Christ who lives in us, is greater than Satan who is in the world. Christ lives in us to give us victory over Satan's temptations, in

Knowing that Christ lives in us and *Trusting* Him to give us the victory.

If there's one thing, I have learned is, when Satan knocks at the door of my heart, to get me to do wrong things, I just say, "Lord Jesus, will you please get the door?" Then when Satan sees the Lord Jesus, Satan bows low and says, "I'm sorry, but I have come to the wrong place." And Satan leaves.

Satan may tempt us, but he can't make us sin. We can say *No* to Satan. In the Bible, it says, in (James 4:7) "Submit yourselves therefore to God. Resist the Devil, and he will flee from you." What happens when we sin? Does God, have a plan to take care of His saved children when they sin? Yes, He does. In (1John 1:9) it says, "If we confess our sins, He is faithful and just to forgive us for our sins, and to cleanse us from all unrighteousness."

What should we do when we sin? We should first of all, confess that sin to God. Then, believe that God forgives us. Now, to confess a sin, means to call it by it's right name and not, make excuses. If we have lied about something, we need to confess to God, that we have lied. Be honest about what you have done wrong.

If we get angry and lost our temper over something, we need to confess this, to God. We should also, make things right with other people. When this is done, we should believe that God has forgiven us.

God wants us to have victory in our lives. The more we learn to trust and obey the Lord Jesus, who lives in us, the more we will be able to say, "No" to the world and the flesh. God gives us victory, through our Lord Jesus Christ. The Bible says, in (1 Corinthians 15:57) "But thanks be to God, which giveth us the victory through our Lord Jesus Christ." Christ won the victory over us, because Christ lives in us, we can all have victory in our lifes. God said it! I believe it! And that settles it! Thank you, Heavenly Father!

Chapter 9

❧

What is the Bible? The Bible is God's Holy Word. It's God's message to us, and it's the most important book in all the world. Okay! The first part of the Bible, is called the Old Testament, and it was written *Before* Christ came to the earth. The second part of the Bible, is called the New Testament, and it was written *After* Christ came to the earth and went back to Heaven.

Now, the Bible has 66 books in it, 39 is in the Old Testament and 27 is in the New Testament. I'm trying as God leads me to keep this as simple as I can.

So, how did we get the Bible? Who wrote the Bible and how did we get it? God Himself, is the true author of the Bible. God told these men what to write and even the words to use. In (ll Peter 1:21) it says, "For the prophecy came not in old time by the will of man, but holy men of God spake as they were moved by the Holy Ghost."

Long ago, God told a man named Jeremiah, to write a part of the Bible. In (Jeremiah 30:2) God said, to Jeremiah, "Thus speaketh the Lord God of Israel, saying, write all the words that I have spoken unto thee in a book." Jeremiah obeyed God and wrote the whole book of Jeremiah. God's Holy Spirit told Jeremiah, exactly what to write, and he wrote every one of the words down.

This is what we mean, when we say that the Bible is "inspired by God." Every book in the Bible was written in this way. In (ll Timothy 3:16) the Bible says, "All scripture is given by inspiration of God, and it's profitable for doctrine, for reproof, for correction, for instruction in righteousness." This is how the Bible was written, and God's Word has been passed down to us from one generation to another.

The Bible is the only book, which was inspired by God. When the last book in the Bible was written God's Word was complete. The Bible warns against adding to the Word of God or taking away from it. After the last, book was written (Revelation), it was a, Revelation.

The Bible says, in (Revelation 22:18-19) "For I testify unto every man that heareth the words of the prophecy of this book. If any man shall add unto these things, God shall add unto him the plagues that are written in this book. And, if any man shall take away this prophecy, God shall take away his part out of the book of life, and out of the Holy City, and from the things which are written in this book." Wow!

So, what's the Bible, about you ask? The Bible tells us how man turned away from God into sin and how God gave His only Son to die for our sins. It, tells us that God loves us and that He wants us to become His children by taking Christ as our Savior.

Your Way is Not God's Way

The Bible is God's love letters to us. The Bible is the most important book in this world, because it tells us how to be saved.

The Apostle Paul, wrote to young Timothy. In (ll Timothy 3:15) it says, "And that from a child thou hast known the holy scriptures, which are able to make thee wise unto Salvation through faith which is in Jesus Christ." Now, God gave us this wonderful book that we might know the *Truth*. The Bible tells us truth about ourselves, about sin, about Satan, Salvation, and about our God.

How can we understand the Bible? There are many things in the Bible that are hard for us all to understand. Wouldn't it be just wonderful if we had a teacher, that knew all about God and His Word? Well, let me tell you, there's someone like that! He's the Holy Spirit! God has given unto us, the Holy Spirit to teach us about the Holy Bible. The very moment we take Christ as our Savior, the Holy Spirit comes to live in us. For He lives in *Every* believer. The Holy Spirit teaches us the things of God. The Lord Jesus said, in (John 14:26) "But the comforter, which is the Holy Ghost, whom the Father will send in my name, he shall teach you all things, and bring all things to your remembrance, whatsoever I have said unto you." So the Holy Spirit, teaches us the things of God. Without the Holy Spirit, we couldn't understand God's Word. How thankful we all should be, that God has given the Holy Spirit to us. Everytime we read the Bible, we should depend on the Holy Spirit to teach us God's Word. This is, what David meant when he prayed, in (Psalms 119:18) "Open thou mine eyes, that I may behold wondrous things out of thy law."

What does God want us to do with the Bible? There are four things God wants us to do:

1-Read the Bible each day. Why? You ask, we should read the Bible, each day, because this is the way God speaks to us and tells us, what He wants us to know and what He wants us to do. Reading the Bible is as important to our spiritual life, as eating food in our physical life. We can't live the Christian life without the Word of God. In (Luke 4:4) The Lord Jesus said, "And Jesus answered him, saying it is written, that man shall not live by bread alone, but by every Word of God."

2-Believe the Bible. We can't please God unless we all have faith. In (Hebrews 11:6) the Bible says, "But without faith it is impossible to please Him,for he that cometh to God must believe that He is, and that He is a rewarder of them that diligently seek Him." So what is faith? Faith is taking God at His Word. Faith is *Believing* the Bible. If, others want to doubt the Bible, let them do so, but right, now settle it in your mind that the Bible *is* God's Holy Word. In (Psalms 119:89) the Bible says, "Forever, O Lord, thy Word is settled in Heaven."

You know I wanted to have more faith. I prayed and prayed, but I didn't seem to have more faith. Then, one day I read this verse in the Bible, in (Romans

10:17) it says, "So then faith cometh by hearing, and hearing by the Word of God." I began to read and study God's Word. As, I read more and studied the Bible more, the more I believed it. And guess what, my faith just grew and grew. Would you like to have more faith? Then read God's Word, believe it and act upon it.

3-Memorize verses from the Bible in "The sword of the spirit." This means, that it's our weapon to use against, Satan. It's so great to know that we have a weapon to use against Satan. In (Ephesians 6:17) it says, "And take the helmet of Salvation, and the sword of the Spirit, which is the Word of God." In (Ephesians 6:18) it says, "Praying always with all power and supplication in the Spirit, and watching there unto with all perseverance and supplication for all saints." When the Lord Jesus, was tempted by Satan in the wilderness, Jesus used the Word of God. Jesus, also memorized the scriptures and He used them to defeat, Satan. Everytime Satan tempted Him, the Lord Jesus said, "It is written." And He quoted a scripture verse, Satan was defeated. You know, it worked for our Lord Jesus, it'll work for us all, also. Thank you, Lord. So, if we want to have victory over Satan's temptations, we must memorize God's Word. One way to look at this is "Hiding God's Word in our heart." In (Psalms 119:11) it says, "Thy Word have I hid in mine heart, that I might not sin against thee." Also, memorizing

God's Word will also, help you to be a great witness for Christ. If you use your own words in talking to others, they might say, "That's just your opinion" or "Who are you to tell me, what I should do or what I shouldn't do?" But, if you quote the Bible, your words will have power, because they are God's Words.

4-Obey the Bible. The Bible contains facts to be believed, our promises to be claimed, and commands, to be obeyed. The Lord wants us to obey Him. Jesus said, in (Matthew 7:21) "Not everyone that saith unto me, Lord, Lord, shall enter unto the Kingdom of Heaven, but he that doeth the will of my Father which is in Heaven." When God tells you, in His Word that you should do something, then *Do It*. God blesses those who obey His Word. The Lord Jesus said, in (Luke 11:28) "But he said, Ye rather, blessed are they that hear the Word of God, and keep it (obey it)."

Begin right now, today and read God's Word each day. Get a Bible with good print and one that you can read easily. Set a time each day to read your Bible, spend time in prayer, also. Most Christians find that the best time to do this, is the first thing in the morning. Whatever works for you, and then do it.

I'd like to begin with the Gospel of John. Now, as you read it, watch for the words, "believe" and "believeth" then underline them in your Bible. It's your Bible, so if it helps you to understand it, by all

Your Way is Not God's Way

means do it. You could also highlight the words and verses. The Gospel of John was written, to help us believe in Jesus Christ, as the Son of God and as our Lord and Savior.

In (John 20:31) John wrote, "But these are written, that ye might believe that Jesus is the Christ, the Son of God, and that believing ye might have life through His name." After you have read the Gospel of John several times, you will want to read the entire New Testament. As you go along, and then read the whole Bible. You'll be so blessed, and so much closer to God for He loves us so, much. When you come across a verse you like, and there'll be many, *Memorize* it.

God promises special blessings to those who love His Words and think about it day and night. When you learn the wonderful truth, from God's Word share it with a friend, and they will be blessed, also. Remember, the most important reason for studying the Bible, is to get to know the Lord Jesus Christ better and to become more like Him. God is my best friend, and He never lets me down. I'm, so thankful for Him. Without Him we're nothing. That's another reason why, I named this book, "**Your Way is Not God's Way**." Our way is nothing, but God's way is everything.

There's three verses I want us to look at from God's Word, it's found, in (l John 5:11-13) it says, "And this is the record, that God hath given to us eternal life, and this life is in His Son." In (Verse 12) it says, "He that hath the Son hath life, and He that hath not the Son of God hath not life." In (Verse

13) it says, "These things have I written unto you that believe on the name of the Son of God, that ye may know that ye have eternal life, and that ye may believe on the name of the Son of God." What do these verses tell us? They tell us what the Bible is "*The record*" of what God has said.

In the Bible, God tells us, that He has given us eternal life, and that this life is in His Son. If you have Christ as your Saviour, you have eternal life, if you don't have Him, you don't have eternal life. A true believer can say, yes, I have eternal life. We *Know*, that we're saved, because God says so, in His Word. How thankful, we all should be for the Word of God! The Bible, is God's Holy Word. God wants us to read, believe, memorize, and obey it!

Now, here are some ideas, that will help you to fellowship, with God as you read the Bible:

1-Why read the Bible? We read the Bible first of all, in order to have fellowship with God. The Bible is God's Word to us. He doesn't speak aloud to us, but He speaks to us in our hearts by His written Word. If we want to hear what God has to say to our hearts, we must read the Bible.
2-How to read the Bible. Read it out loud. It'll help to keep your mind on what you're reading.
3-*Think* and don't be in a big hurry. Take time to think, about what you are reading.
4-Talk to God. Talk to Him about what you are reading. When you don't understand something, tell Him so and ask Him to help you

to understand. When you read something wonderful about God, tell Him right then, how wonderful He is.

5- Wait on God. This simply means, to be quiet, before God, with your mind on Him and His Word.

6- *Mark It*. When God speaks something special to you, always underline it or highlight those words in your Bible. That's God's Word to you, personally.

7- *Obey It*. Do what God tells you to do. Sometimes, He shows us a sin, that we need to confess to Him. Sometimes, He shows us something that needs to be made right, with another person. Always be quick to obey God's spoken Words.

8- *Say It*. Share with others the blessings that God gives you as you read His Word. It'll also, help others and it'll help you, also.

9- *Remember It*. All through the day, let your mind go back to the Word, that God spoke to you. Talk to Him, about what's on your heart. This is a wonderful fellowship that we have with God. One amazing thing about the Bible, is that it tells us about the future.

Chapter 10

❧

God knows the future, and in His Word, He has told us many things that are going to happen. Perhaps one thing you have been wondering about is this, "Will the Lord Jesus ever come to this earth again?" The answer is…Yes, yes, yes, He will.

The Lord Jesus said, in (John 14:2-3) "In my Fathers house are many mansions, if it were not so, I would have told you. I go to prepare a place for you." In (Verse 3) it says, "And, if I go and prepare a place for you, *I Will Come Again*, and receive you unto myself, that where I am, there ye may be also." Jesus is coming again. Oh glory! The Lord Jesus, did many wonderful things while He was on this earth, but the main reason He came was to die for us. The Lord Jesus, was crucified about nine o'clock in the morning. He died about three O'clock that afternoon. A man named Joseph, of Arimathaea, asked for the body of Jesus. He and a friend named Nicodemus, tenderly prepared the body of Jesus, for burial. They wrapped His body in linen clothes with spices. Then they placed Jesus' body in a new tomb carved in the side of a hill. A big, large stone was rolled across the entrance. Jesus was dead. The disciples were very, sad. Even though Jesus had told them, "He would rise again from the dead, on the third day," they just didn't really believe it at the time. Oh! What a day that must have been, early in the morning of the third day, three women came to the tomb of Jesus, to put spices on His body. When they arrived at the tomb, they were stunned, as they found, that the heavy stone had been rolled away, from the entrance.

An angel spoke to them and said, in (Matthew 28:5-6) "And the angel answered and said unto the women, Fear not ye, for I know that ye seek Jesus, which was crucified." In (Verse 6) it says, "He is not here, for He is risen, as He said. Come, see the place where the Lord lay." The women saw that the body of Jesus was really no longer in the tomb. *Wow!* They were frightened and puzzled. They ran off to tell the Disciples.

When Mary Magdalene met with Peter and John, she told them what had happened, and Peter and John ran to the tomb to see for themselves. They too, found the tomb completely empty except for the grave clothes. Jesus rose from the grave.

Later on, Mary returned to the tomb. As she, was standing outside the tomb weeping, the Lord Jesus appeared to her. In her sorrow, she thought, He was a gardener. So she said, to Him "Sir, if thou hast borne Him, hence tell me where thou hast laid Him." Jesus said, "Mary". When she turned and she recognized Him, she exclaimed and said, "Master!"

That night, ten of the Disciples met in a closed room. They were talking about all of the strange things that had happened that day. Suddenly, Jesus appeared in their midst. In (Luke 24:38-39) it says, "And He said unto them, why are ye troubled? And why do thoughts arise in your hearts?" In (Verse 39) it says, "Behold my hands and my feet, that it is *I* myself, handle me, and see, for a spirit hath not flesh and bones, as ye see me have." *Oh Glory*, the Lord Jesus had arisen from the grave, in His body of flesh and bones.

Now, here's a question, how did the Disciples know that He had a body? Simple, they saw Him, they touched Him, they talked with Him, and they ate with Him. Jesus was alive. They couldn't hardly wait to tell the wonderful news of His resurrection to Thomas, who wasn't in the closed room with the other Ten Disciples. When they told Thomas, he just didn't believe them.

In (John 20:25) Thomas said, "The other Disciples therefore said unto Him, we have seen the Lord. But He said unto them, Except I shall see in His hands the print of the nails, and put my finger into the print of the nails, and thrust my hand into His side, I will not believe." Well, eight days later, the Disciples were again, in the same closed room. But, this time Thomas was with them. Again, the Lord Jesus appeared to them and said, "Peace be unto you." Then the Lord Jesus said, to Thomas, "Reach hither, thy finger, and behold my hands, and reach hither thy hand, and thrust it into my side, and be not faithless, but believing." Thomas didn't doubt any longer.

For he, worshipped Jesus saying, "My Lord and my God." The Lord Jesus said, "Thomas, because thou has seen me, thou hast believed, blessed are they that have not seen, and yet have believed."

The Lord Jesus, appeared on earth for forty days after His resurrection. He was seen by many, many people. On one occasion, he appeared to over 500 believers at one single time. Wow, that must have been so amazing!

Before, the Lord Jesus went back to Heaven, in (Matthew 28:18) Jesus said, to His Disciples, "And Jesus came and spake unto them, saying, All power is given unto me in Heaven and in earth." Then one day, when the Disciples were with Him, the Lord Jesus was taken from them. A cloud received Him out of their sight. Jesus had gone back to Heaven.

While they stood looking toward the sky, two men in white clothing stood by them and said, "Ye men of Galilee, why stand ye gazing up into Heaven? This same Jesus, which is taken up from you into Heaven, shall so come in like manner as ye have seen Him go into Heaven."

This verse is saying, in (Acts 1:11) "the *Lord Jesus Will* come again," in the very same way in which He went back to Heaven. The Disciples saw Jesus go back to Heaven, and *"All Believers"* who are living, when Jesus comes again, will see Him at that time. You know, that's something I just can't wait to happen, to meet the Lord Jesus face to face, and you know, I'll give Him a very big hug, also. What a day that will be. Glory to His name. For the Lord Jesus is preparing beautiful mansions in Heaven for us all, and one day He is coming back to take us to be with Him.

In (John 14:2-3) it says, "In my Father's house are many mansions, if it were not so, I would have told you. I go to prepare a place for you." In (Verse 3) it says, "And if I go and prepare a place for you, I will come again, and receive you unto myself, that where I am, there ye may be also." We know He is coming because He said, "I will come again." For those of us who have received Him as our Savior, His coming will be a time of great joy. Why? Because, He's coming to take us, to be with Him.

Here's what the Bible tells us about that glorious day. It says in, (l Thessalonians 4:16-17) "For the Lord Himself shall descend from Heaven with a shout, with the voice of archangel, and with the trump of God, and the dead in Christ shall rise first." In (Verse 17) it says, "Then we which are alive and remain shall be caught up together with them in the clouds, to meet the Lord in the air, and so shall we ever be with the Lord." *Glory! Glory! Glory!*

I've kept it simple, so, we all can understand that the believers, who have died and the believers, who are living on earth, when Jesus does come, we will be taken up together, to meet Him in the clouds. What a happy, time this will be. I know I'll see you there in Heaven. Of course, our bodies will be changed and we'll be made like His resurrected body. Jesus is coming for His believers.

What about those, who have never taken Christ as their Savior? They will be left behind. There'll be a time of great trouble on the earth for them. Jesus said, "For then, shall be great tribulation, such as was not since the beginning of the world." This is just how important it is, for us to win as many as we can to Christ right, now. After these events, the Lord Jesus, will return to the earth with His believers. All those who have been with Him in Heaven will return with Him to reign with Him.

Right now, I feel so close to our God. Through God, I know I'm writing what He wants me to write. I feel His great power all over me, it's so great I'm trembling as I write. I, pray Dear Lord, *"take this material I'm writing and apply it to everyone's hearts that's going to read it. Bless them Lord from the tip of their heads to the bottom of their feet." God, your will be done, in your Holy Name, I pray, hold your people, you know our hearts. For we know Heavenly Father, that through you, all things are possible. In Jesus name, I pray."* Amen and Amen.

First, He'll come for us, and then He returns, with us. What a great and wonderful time this will be. We all ask, "When is Jesus coming? Does anyone know?" No! No man, knows exactly when the Lord Jesus will come again. But I promise, it won't be long now.

In (Matthew 24:36) Jesus said, "But of that day and hour knoweth no man, no, not the Angels of Heaven, but my Father only." Jesus may come at anytime. Since, this is so very true, we should be ready to meet Him at all times. How can we be ready, for the coming of Lord Jesus? We can be ready for His coming by

1-Loving Him.
2-Obeying Him.
3-Serving Him.
4-Looking for His return.

If we do these things, we won't be ashamed, before Him when He comes.

In (1 John 2:28) the Bible says, "And now, little children, abide in Him, that when He shall appear, we may have confidence, and not be ashamed before Him at His coming." If we truly love the Lord Jesus, we will want Him to come very,soon.

In (Revelation 22:20) it says, "He which testifieth these things saith, surely I come quickly. Amen. Even so, come, Lord Jesus." Let's let this be our prayer everyday. Jesus is coming soon! We must be ready when He does come.

What happens when a Christian dies? The Bible tells us, that the body is the "house" in which the soul lives. Our body isn't really, us, it's just the house in which our soul lives. We can, understand this because we live in a house. The house isn't us, it's just a place where we live. Our soul simply moves out of the house, in which it has lived and goes to be with the, Lord.

The Apostle Paul said, "For me to live, is Christ and to die, is gain." Why did He say that it was "*Gain*" to die? Because to die, is to be with Christ, and this, my friend, is far better than being here. When, a Christians loved one dies, we are sorrowful because we miss them. This is natural, but we must remember, that they're with Jesus. The soul goes to

Christ, and our body goes to sleep in Jesus. If only, we could see how beautiful Heaven is, we would never want to bring our loved ones back here.

We, don't have to fear death. As a Christian, the Bible calls death simply, "falling asleep in Jesus." The Lord Jesus said, in (John 11:25) "Jesus said unto her, I am the resurrection, and the life, he that believeth in me, though he were dead, yet shall he live."

When Jesus comes again, He will raise the bodies of those who belong to Him, and He will give them new resurrected bodies, which can never die. The Bible says, in (ll Corinthians 5:1) "For we know that if our earthly house of this tabernacle were dissolved, we have a building of God, resurrected a house not made with hands, eternal in the Heavens."

What will we be like then? We shall be like Jesus. The Bible says, in (l John 3:2) "Beloved, now are we the Sons of God, and it doth not yet appear what we shall be, but we know that, when He shall appear, we shall be like Him, for we shall see Him as He is."

Chapter 11

❧

Did you ever receive a reward for doing well on your report card? Our God, gives us rewards to His children, for the good things they do. God doesn't give rewards to unsaved people, but only to His own saved children. It will help us understand Salvation and rewards, if we see, that there are *Two* differences between them.

    1-Salvation is free, but rewards are *Earned*.
    2-We have Salvation *Now*, but rewards will be given *Later*, when we get to Heaven.

Salvation is a gift and you have it, now. Rewards must be earned, and they'll be given out when we get to Heaven. The question is, how do we earn rewards? We earn them by faithfully serving Christ. Those who have been saved, may earn wonderful rewards, by the work they do for the Lord. The Bible speaks of some very special rewards, for those who faithfully serve the Lord Jesus. They are called, "*Crowns*." Crowns speak of Glory, reigning with the Lord Jesus.

Your Way is Not God's Way

There're 5 beautiful crowns, which will be given to believers, as rewards that are mentioned in the Bible.

1- In (l Thessalonians 2:19-20) it says, "For what is your hope, or joy, or crown of rejoicing? Are not even ye in the presence of our Lord Jesus Christ at His coming?" In (Verse 20) it says, "For ye are our glory and joy." This is the crown of rejoicing for those who win others to Christ. Sometimes, it's called the soul-winners crown.
2- In (ll Timothy 4:8) it says, "Henceforth there is laid up for me a crown of righteousness, which the Lord, the righteous judge, shall give me at that day, and not to me only, but unto all them also that love His appearing." This is the crown of righteousness, for those who look for and love Christ's return.
3- In (l Peter 5:4) it says, "And when the chief Shepherd shall appear, ye shall receive a crown of glory that fadeth not away." This is the crown of glory, for those who faithfully teach and preach God's Word.
4- In (l Corinthians 9:25) it says, "And, every man that striveth for the mastery is temperate in all things. Now, they do it to obtain a corruptible crown, but we an incorruptible." This is the incorruptible crown for those who run a good race, in the Christian life.
5- In (Revelation 2:10) it says, "Fear none of those things which thou shall suffer, behold,

the Devil shall cast some of you into prison, that ye may be tried, and ye shall have tribulation ten days, be thou faithful into death, and I will give thee crown of life." This is the crown of life, for those who suffer, for the name of Christ, especially those who lay down their lives for Him. We, receive eternal life by simply trusting Christ as our Savior. We receive the crown of life, by being faithful. So, these are the five beautiful crowns, which will be given to believers as rewards.

This is what happens, if we don't live for the Lord, if we live for ourselves and don't serve the Lord Jesus, we will not receive any rewards at all. Instead, we'll be ashamed, when we stand before the Lord.

Perhaps you are saying to yourself, "I want to live a life that's pleasing to the Lord, but how can I know whether or not, I should do a certain thing?" We should see what God says about it in the Bible. God tells us that we shouldn't curse, or lie, steal, we should forgive people in our hearts. Therefore, we know that we shouldn't do these things. You know, you are doing right through God, even though no one is watching you, always remember that our Heavenly Father, is always watching us. Ask yourself, "Would Jesus like to see me doing this? If you think that He wouldn't like for you to do it, then don't do it.

You ask, "What will happen to the child of God, who continues to do things that aren't pleasing to God? Let me tell you, God will chasten you. In

(Hebrews 12:6) it says, "For whom the Lord loveth He chasteneth, and scourgeth every son whom he receiveth." A good father chastens or corrects his child, when he does wrong. Does God, chasten His child because He hates him or because He loves him? Well, of course He does it because He loves him. We love God, because He loves us. Our, Heavenly Father is a good father. He, loves us too much, to let us go in disobedience, ruining our lives and bringing shame to His name.

God will speak to our hearts, when we do wrong, if we don't listen to Him and turn from our disobedience, He will surely chasten us. Now, how does God chasten us? He does so, by letting trouble come into our lifes, and we know we have more than enough troubles already, in our lives without, adding more to it. When our Heavenly Father chastens us, let's remember, He does this because He loves us. All Christians will be judged.

By now, I'm sure that you have realized, just how very important you live, your life as a Christian. The Bible says, that one day we must stand before the Lord Jesus, to be judged. Every believer will be judged for the things they did, after they were saved, whether good or bad. This judgment is called, "The Judgment Seat of Christ."

The Bible says, in (II Corinthians 5:10) "For we must all appear before the judgment seat of Christ, that everyone may receive the things done in his body, according to that he hath done, whether it be good or bad." This judgment isn't to see whether or not we'll go to Heaven. *Every* believer will go to Heaven. This judgment is for rewards. If we faithfully served the Lord Jesus, this will be a time of great rejoicing for us, because we'll receive wonderful rewards. If we, have lived for the good times, of this world, instead of living for the Lord Jesus, we will be ashamed. Perhaps, some of us will wish, we could live our lives over again, but that won't be possible. The time to live for the Lord Jesus, is *Right Now*. The time to serve Him is now. Only, one life, it will soon be past. Only what is done for Christ will last.

In (Romans 6:23) it says, "For the wages of sin is death, but the gift of God is eternal life through Jesus Christ our Lord." In (Ephesians 2:8-9) it says, "For by grace are ye saved through faith, and that not of yourselves, it is the gift of God." In (Verse 9) it says, "Not of works, lest any man should boast." Salvation is a free gift, but rewards are earned, by faithful service.

Do, you know some people who don't know Christ, as their Savior? Would you like to win them for Him? Start by praying for them. Tell them, about our Savior. When prayers go up to Heaven, answers and blessings, come down from Heaven. For if you win them to Christ, you shall receive the soul winners crown. And, you'll shine as the stars in Heaven, for ever and ever.

The Bible says, in (Daniel 12:3) "And they that be wise shall shine as the brightness of the firmament, and they that turn many to righteousness as the stars for ever and ever."

Chapter 12

❦

We'll, never understand what the Christian life is all about, until we see, that it involves spiritual welfare. There are two Kingdoms that are at war, God's Kingdom and Satan's Kingdom. The battle is for the souls of men. Do we have a part in this warfare? You bet, we do, our part is to be soldiers, that God can use in the battle against Satan. Now, what kind of weapons do we use, in the warfare with Satan? We use *Spiritual* weapons. It's the greatest weapon God has given to us is, *Prayer*. Why? Because prayer releases God's power.

In (Jeremiah 33:3) God said, "Call unto me, and I will answer thee, and shew the great and mighty things, which thou knowest not." We must pray. We, simply can't live the Christian life without prayer. It's through prayer, that we commune with God. It's through prayer that we intercede for others, and it's through prayer, that we *Bind* the power of Satan. God uses our prayers, in the battle against Satan, through our prayers. Through our prayers, we can touch the world for God.

But, first let's consider some very important things about prayer. Now, what is a prayer? Plain and simple, prayer is talking with God. Prayer is a ritual or a public performance, it's a very personal matter, between you and God. The Lord Jesus said, "When, thou prayest, enter into thy closet and when thou hast shut the door, pray to thy Heavenly Father in secret." The Lord Jesus, told us not to use "vain repetitions" meaning, saying the same things over and over. Our prayers must be sincere and from the heart.

Now, to whom do we pray? The Lord Jesus said, in (Matthew 6:9) "After this manner therefore pray ye, our Father which art in Heaven, hollowed be thy name." Can everyone pray to God as the Father? *No*, only those who are in God's family can call Him "*Father.*" There's only one prayer that God, will hear from an unsaved person, it's the prayer asking, for forgiveness. Our, God always hears this prayer, from an unsaved person. This is so important. We must pray in Jesus name. Because, if we want God to answer our prayers, we must pray in the name of, Jesus.

The Lord Jesus said, in (John 16:23) "And in that day ye shall ask me nothing. Verily, verily I say unto you, whosoever ye shall ask the Father in my name, He will give it you."

The Lord Jesus, is our greatest intercessor in Heaven. We pray to the Father in His name. It's because of who Jesus is and what He has done, that God hears and answers our prayers, also the Holy Spirit helps us, pray. We, not only have a intercessor in Heaven, but we also have one in our hearts, being the" Holy Spirit." For, He helps us to pray.

You know, many times we don't know God's will, about a matter, and therefore we don't know how to pray, about it. But, the Holy Spirit knows the mind of God and He helps us to pray according to God's will. The Bible says, in (Romans 8:26) "Likewise the Spirit also helpeth our infirmities, for we know not what we should pray for, as we ought, but the Spirit itself maketh intercession for us with groaning, which can't be uttered."

In (Romans 8:27) it says, "And, He that searcheth the hearts knoweth what is the mind of the Spirit, because He maketh intercession for the saints according to the will of God."

In (Romans 8:28) it says, "And we know that all things work together for good to them that love God, to them who are the called according to his purpose."

Does prayer really influence God's actions? *Yes*, of course it does. How do we know? Because God says, so. The Lord Jesus said, in (John 14:14) "If ye shall ask any thing in my name, I will do it." Also, in (John 14:13) it says, "And whatsoever ye shall ask in my name, that will I do, that the Father may be glorified in the Son." Then, in (John 14:12) it says, "Verily, verily, I say unto you, He that believeth on me, the works that I do shall he do also, and greater works than these shall He do, because I go unto my Father."

In these verses, the Lord tells us plainly that His doing, depends upon our asking. Remember this, in

(James 4:2) it says,"Ye lust, and you have not: ye kill, and desire to have, and can not obtain: ye fight and war, yet ye have not, because ye ask not." For God is omnipotent-meaning, He can do anything, He chooses to do. But, God has chosen to use our prayers, in accomplishing His work here on earth. Now, do you see how very important prayer really is? Prayer isn't just for asking. There's three forms of prayer:

1-Communion.
2-Petition.
3-Intercession.

Now, let me explain, these three important prayers.

1-*Communion*-This is fellowship with God. We read God's Word, so that He can speak to us, then we go to Him in prayer. We worship Him, we adore Him, we praise Him, we thank Him for His blessings and we tell Him how much we love Him. Communion also includes confession, for we can't commune with God, if we have unconfessed, sin in our life. Communion with God is absolutely essential. It's through communion, with God, that we came to know Him and experience His power. The Bible says, "The people that do know their God, shall be strong and do exploits."

2-*Petition*-Is asking God for what we need. And, we need many, many things, for sure we need strength to overcome temptation. We need wisdom. We need power to serve God effectively. We need guidance in making everyday decisions. We need food, clothes, and a lot of other necessities.

Where should we look for the supply of our needs? We should always look to God. He's our Heavenly Father. He loves us, and He delights to have us come to Him with our needs. The Lord Jesus said, in (Matthew 7:11) "If ye then, being evil, know how to give good gifts unto your children, how much more shall your Father which is in Heaven give good things to them that ask Him?"

When you need something, just ask God for it. And, keep on asking, often we lack things simply because we haven't asked God for it. Does God always answer prayers? *No,* God doesn't *Always* answer our prayers. There are two conditions which we must meet if we want God to answer out prayers.

1-We must pray in the will of God. If we ask God, for something that's not in accord with His will, He will not give it to us. We should be very grateful for this, because we don't always know what is best for us.

For instance, a child might ask his father for a razor or a sharp knife, but of course the father, loves his child and he knows that this would bring pain and suffering to him. Therefore, he doesn't grant his child's request. The greatest prayer we can pray to God is, "Thy will be done." This shows that we are trusting God's love and His wisdom. We, can ask for the things we want, but in all of our prayers,we should pray, *"Thy Will Be Done."*

In (l John 5:14) says, "And, this is the confidence that we have in Him, that, if we ask any thing according to His will, He heareth us." In (John 5:15) it says, "And, if we know that He hears us, whatsoever we ask, we know that we have the petitions that we desired of Him."

2-We must be "on playing ground." This means that our life must be pleasing to God. God doesn't answer the prayers, of worldly and disobedient, Christians. But, He delights to answer the prayers, of those whose lives are pleasing to Him.

The Bible says, in (l John 3:21-22) "Beloved, if our hearts condemn us not, then have we confidence toward God." In (l John 3:22) it says, "And whatsoever we ask, we receive of Him, because we keep His commandments, and do those things that are pleasing to His sight." When, our prayers aren't answered, we should ask ourselves, is there anything in my life, that's hindering God, from answering my prayers? The great hindrances to prayer, are:

1-Sin.
2-Selfishness.
3-Unforgiveness.
4-Disbelief.

These things give Satan a foothold in our life, and God will not hear our prayers. In (Psalms 66:18) it says, "If I regard iniquity in my heart, the Lord will not hear me." And, in (Psalms 66:19) it says, "But verily God hath heard me, He hath attended to the voice of my prayer."

3-*Intercession*-This is a prayer for others, communion and petition, are mainly for our needs, but intercession reaches out to help others. We, pray for our unsaved friends and relatives, leaders, and those who are sick. Now, this form of prayer helps God in His great love plan, to bring, men and women back to Him.

One form of intercession is prayer, "warfare." This is prayer against Satan. When, we have learned how to keep in touch with God, through prayer and the reading of His Word, then, God can and will use us in the battle against, Satan.

Now, let's stop and review some facts concerning the warfare between God and Satan:

1-God created this earth, it belongs to Him. The Bible says, in (Psalms 24:1) "The earth is the Lord's, and the fullness thereof, the world, and they that dwell therein."
2-God gave the rulership of this earth to man. God, gave Adam dominion over all the earth.
3-Adam rebelled against God. He took sides with Satan and came under the power of Satan. Therefore, Adam lost the rulership of the world,

and Satan took it over. It was through sin, that Satan gained full control over the world.

4-God wants to bring this world back to Himself. And, He wanted to do it through us. So, God sent His son, the Lord Jesus Christ, into the world as His second man.

5-A great battle raged between Satan and the Lord Jesus, God's second man. The Lord Jesus, was tempted but He was victorious over all the temptations of Satan. Finally, in desperation, Satan stirred up people to crucify, Jesus.

When the Lord Jesus lay in the tomb, Satan of course thought he had won the victory. But, on the third day, *oh glory*! Our, Lord Jesus arose from the dead. Victor over all the powers of darkness. Satan knew then, that he was defeated. Christ defeated *All* the powers of darkness. The Lord was given all authority in Heaven and earth. Satan, and his forces of darkness, were stripped of their authority. The Lord Jesus ascended back into Heaven. Where, He is seated at the right hand, of the Father. Far above all principality, power, might and dominion. We can claim Christ's victory over Satan. Now, a great thing to remember, is in our warfare against Satan, is this, *Satan Is Defeated*. So, we don't have to defeat Satan, our Christ has already defeated him at Calvary. Though Satan is defeated, he has not yet been cast into the lake of fire, where he belongs. For the time being, he's free, and he's working very hard, to keep unsaved people in his Kingdom.

As Gods servants, you and I, are to proclaim the Gospel to the unsaved and to deliver them from Satan's, gripping power. For the Lord Jesus said, "that if you want to take goods from the house of a strong man, you must first bind the strong man." Satan, is the strong man, and his goods, are the people, he holds in his power. If, we're to deliver people from Satan's power, we must first *Bind* his power.

Now, how do we bind Satan's power? We do so by, *Claiming Christ's Victory Of Calvery*. Glory! Now, we come to a very important question, how do we make Christ's Victory, "*Our*" Victory? We make His Victory, ours, by *Claiming* it. Christ paid for our sins on the cross, but you <u>were</u> <u>not</u> saved until you claimed it. You, must claim Christ's, Victory over Satan. You can do this by praying, "All that Calvary means, Lord! All the mighty victory of Calvary!" When you pray this prayer, you are saying, "Lord I can't deal with this situation, but, you can. You're victorious over all the power of Satan, and I'm claiming your Victory in this matter." In the name of Jesus. As we claim the Victory of Calvary, Christ binds the power of Satan. Now, use the weapons God has given to you. God has given you a mighty weapon, to use against, Satan. But, a weapon isn't any good, unless you use it. So, claim the Victory of Calvary.

These are hard words and bitter feelings. What should you do? Claim the Victory of Calvary, everytime Satan comes at you, just claim the Victory of Calvary, and send Satan, away from you. Christ says, to you "Bind the strong man, Satan, in my name." All that Calvary means:

1-Our sins are paid for.
2-The power of darkness is defeated.
3-Christ exalted.
4-Bind the power of Satan.

The Kingdom of darkness (*sin*). We passed out of the Kingdom of darkness, by our death with Christ. We're no longer under the authority of sin. We're in the Kingdom of God's Son. Thank you, Lord Jesus.

You know, we often have problems, we try to deal with people, we think are causing the problems, but the Bible says, that the real difficulty is with the powers of darkness, stirring up the matters. The Apostle Paul said, in (Ephesians 6:12) "For we wrestle not against flesh and blood, but against principalities, against powers, against the rulers of the darkness of this world, against spiritual wickedness in high places."

In (Ephesians 6:13) it says, "Wherefore, take unto you, the whole armour of God, that ye may be able to understand in the evil day, and having done all, to stand."

How do we deal with the powers of darkness? We, deal with them by claiming Christ's, Victory of Calvary. "All the mighty power of Calvary, Victory in Jesus, name." When you understand that, we're at war with Satan, you'll have to pray about everything. For this, is the greatest thing you can do for God or man. Pray about problems in your home and in your Church. Pray for all Christians. Pray for all unsaved friends and relatives. And, pray for those who are preaching the Gospel. Pray in Jesus's name. Pray with earnestly. Pray with belief. Pray in the victory of Calvary. And don't give up. The winning quality in prayer is persistence. This means *"Don't Give Up."* Keep praying, until your answer comes. It takes time for God to deal with human, wills. It takes time to change situations. Our God, wants us to hold on, in prayer, claiming the Victory of Calvary. The Lord Jesus said, "Men ought always to pray, and not to faint." Remember God's promise: *If You Ask, I Will Do.*

1-As believers, we have our discharge from serving sin. The Bible says, "He that hath died is freed from sin." He has, His discharge. God says, to you, "you have your discharge from serving sin." Now, count on this fact and claim your freedom. Don't let sin reign over you, anymore. You must obey God. When sin comes to you, say to it, "I recognize your presence and your power, but I refuse to obey you." On the basis of God's clear Word, I count myself dead, to you, through Jesus Christ, my Lord. You shall *Not* rule over me. This is taking God at His Word. This breaks the power of sin in your life.

2-Count on Christ's life in you. Temptation comes to all of us, not only from Satan, but also from within ourselves. The Bible says, in (James 1:14) "But every man is tempted, when he is drawn away from his own lust, and enticed." In (James 1:15) it states, "Then, when lust hath conceived, it bringeth forth sin, and sin, when it's finished, bringeth forth death." We have within us, something which is always, trying to pull us back into sin. The Bible calls it, "the law of sin, which is in our members."

Okay, what is law? A law is something that happens over and over. For instance, we speak of the law of gravity. What, do we mean by this? It means, that there's a force, that always causes an object to fall to the ground, when it's released. So, no matter where you go, this happens, so we call it the law of gravity.

We have within us, a sin principle, which is always trying to pull us back into sin. *That's* why the Bible, calls it the law of sin. Can, we overcome the law of sin, by our own efforts? I'm afraid the answer is *No*. God must deliver us, from sins power. God delivers, us by giving us, Christ. His life overcomes the law of sin and death in us.

Let's go back to the law of gravity, again. We know, that the law of gravity is always operating. It holds us fast to the ground. We can't fly, without some mechanical device. Okay, what about birds, birds can fly. Does this mean that the law of gravity doesn't apply to them? *No*. The law of gravity pulls them downward, just as it does us. But, birds have a kind of life that overcomes the law of gravity. The law of a bird's life is to fly.

Okay, now, let's go back to our situation. We, have the law of sin in our members, but we also have Christ living in us, and there is a law to His life. The law of Christ's life, is to overcome sin. His life *Always* triumphs over sin. And, His life is overcomes the law of sin and death.

The Bible says, in (Romans 8:2) "For the law of the Spirit of life in Christ Jesus hath made me free from the law of sin and death." And, in (Romans 8:3) it says, "For what the law couldn't do, in that it was weak through the flesh, God sending His own Son in the likeness of sinful flesh, and for sin, condemned sin in the flesh." This is so wonderful, but now, there's one condition which we must meet, if we want Christ's life to overcome sin in us. We, must *Trust* Him to do this.

> 3-Arm yourself with the *Word Of God*. We, know about the mighty weapon of prayer, which God has given to us, but God has given to us another weapon to use against Satan. This weapon is the Word of God. The Bible says, in (Ephesians 6:17) "And take the helmet of Salvation, and the sword of the Spirit, which is the Word of God." And in, (Ephesians 6:19) it says, "And for me, that utterance may be given unto me, that I may open my mouth boldly, to make known the mystery of the Gospel." When, the Lord Jesus, was tempted in the wilderness, He used this weapon to defeat Satan. Three times, Satan tempted the Lord Jesus and three times, Jesus answered him with the Word of God. The

Lord Jesus, used exactly the right verse to meet each temptation of, Satan. When Satan tried to get Jesus to worship him, by offering Him all the Kingdoms of this world. Jesus didn't quote the 23rd Psalms to him. This is a very beautiful passage of scripture, but it wasn't the weapon to use against that temptation. Instead, Jesus said, "Get thee hence, Satan, for *it is* written, thou shalt worship the Lord thy God, and Him only shalt thou serve."

Our Lord Jesus, defeated Satan, because He had memorized the Word of God, and He knew how to use it. Do you see why, it's so important for you and I memorize scriptures? We must arm ourselves with the *Word Of God*.

Here are some Victory verses the Lord has put on my heart for us to learn, what they mean, and help to memorize them, to use against Satan.

In (John 8:32) it says, "Ye shall know the truth, and the truth, shall make you free." God's Word is the truth. When, you know the truth about sin, Satan, and temptation, you can be set free, from their power over you.

In (Romans 6:14) it says, "For sin shall not have dominion over you, for ye are not under the law, but under Grace." Sin shall not continue to rule over you. Why? Because you are under grace, where God's mighty power works in your behalf. Christ lives in you. He'll enable you to overcome sins power.

In (James 4:7) it says, "Submit yourselves therefore to God. Resist the Devil, and he will flee from you." Learn to resist Satan, resist him with the Word of God. Resist him in Jesus' name. Resist him in the Victory of Calvary. Remind, Satan that he's defeated and tell him to leave you alone.

In (l John 4:4) it says, "Ye are of God, little children, and have overcome them, because greater is "He" that is in you, than He that is in the world." Jesus Christ, is the one who is in you. Satan is the one who is in the world. This verse says, that Jesus Christ who is in you, is greater than Satan who is in the world.

In (ll Timothy 1:7) it says, "For God hath not given us the spirit of fear, but of power, and of love, and of a sound mind." The spirit of fear is from, Satan. Don't accept it. God, doesn't give us the spirit of fear, instead, He gives, us the spirit of power, love and of a sound mind. Oh! Thank you, Lord Jesus.

In (Philippians 1:6) it says, "Being confident of this very thing, that He which hath begun a good work in you will perform it until the day of Jesus Christ." If you're God's child, God has begun a good work in you. He'll continue that work, until the day you go meet Him in Heaven. That's something you can count on.

In (Philippians 4:13) it says, "I can do all things through Christ which strengtheneth me." The Lord Jesus, gives me strength to do whatever He wants me to do. Why? Because He lives in me, and he's the one who does it. In (Ephesians 6:10) it says, "Be strong in the Lord, and in the power of His might." We're not going to be strong in ourselves, but we are to be strong in the Lord. This means, that we're to count on Him and His mighty power to give us Victory.

In (Romans 8:31) says, "What shall we then say to these things? If, God be for us, who can be against us?" Child of God, God is for you. You can be sure of this, because He says so. Since God is for you, it doesn't matter who's against you.

In (Romans 8:28) "And, we know that all things work together for good to them that love God, to them who are the called according to His purpose." Some, things taken by themselves may not seem good to us, but we know God is working, *All* things together for the good, of the person who truly loves Him. We can, know this because God says, so.

4-Make *No* provision for the flesh. To overcome temptation. we must not make any provision for the flesh. This means, that you must not do things or get into situations that make it easy for you to sin.

In (Romans 13:14) says, "But put ye on the Lord Jesus Christ, and make not provision for the flesh, to fulfill the lust thereof." Here,are some suggestions that will help you to overcome temptations. Avoid friends and companions, who lead you to do the wrong things.

Believe me, that's how, when I was younger, I got myself into alot of trouble. Learn, how to say "*No.*" The Bible, in (Proverbs1:10) it says, "My son, if sinners entice thee, consent thou not."

Be very careful of what you look at. You can't help from seeing some evil things, but it's the second look, that can lead to sin. Guard your thought life. A clean mind is priceless.

You, can't have a clean mind, if you read dirty magazines and look at dirty movies. Don't allow evil thoughts to remain in your mind. You, may not be able to keep Satan, from putting an evil thought into your mind, but you can stop it, immediately. As, someone told me sometime ago, "you can't keep the birds from flying over your head, but you can keep them from nesting in your hair." Fill your mind with God's Word.

The Bible says, in (Psalms 119:11) "Thy Word have I hid in mine heart, that I might not sin against thee." Know your weak points. For Satan sure does. Guard these areas of your life especially. One of the best ways to handle sexual temptation is to *Run* from it. This is what Joseph, did when he was tempted by an evil woman. Don't go to any place, where you wouldn't want to be, in, when Jesus comes. Don't do anything, that you wouldn't want to be doing, when Jesus comes.

Confess sin immediately. Don't remain in defeat. Look at the Lord to deliver you from temptation. The Psalmist said, in (Psalms 25:15) "Mine eyes are ever toward the Lord, for He shall pluck my feet out of the net." Don't be deceived by Satan. The Bible says, "*Every* good gift and *Every* perfect gift is from above." If, it's *not* from God, it'*s* sin. Recognize it as such and refuse it.

In (James 1:15) it says, "Then when lust hath conceived, it bringeth forth sin, and sin, when it's finished bringeth forth death." God has given us a wonderful promise, and every Christian, should memorize this verse found, in (1 Corinthians 10:13) it says, "There hath no temptation taken you, but such as in common to man, but God is faithful, who will not suffer you to be tempted above that ye are able, but will with the temptation also make a way to escape, that ye may be able to bear it." What does this verse say? It says, that other people are tempted with the same things, that tempt you. But, God is faithful. Meaning, that you can count on Him, to do what He says, He will do. What does God promise here? He promises, that He won't allow you to be tempted, above what you are able to bear. He, promises to make a way of escape for you, so that you don't have to sin. You can have Victory over every temptation. God said, "Sin shall not have dominion over you."

Remember these four things:

1-Count on your death with Christ.
2-Count on Christ's life in you.
3-Arm yourself with the Word of God.
4-Make no provisions for the flesh.

Well, I sure hope and pray, this material, will help you with your Salvation and in defeating Satan's temptations. Through our God, *all* things are possible.

Chapter 13

☙❦☙

Thank you, Lord Jesus, I hope and pray, that the people that are reading this book, that the Lord has laid on my heart, are receiving as much of a blessing as I am, writing it. Oh glory! It's blessings, all around, again. Thank you, Lord Jesus. All these blessings and wonderful things are called "the mercies of God."

We deserved nothing but death, but God has freely bestowed all of these great blessings on us. Now, God has asked us to do something for Him. What is it, that God's asked us to do? God has asked us to *Consecrate* ourselves to Him.

Let's, hear what God says, to us, through His servant, Paul. In (Romans 12:1) it says, "I beseech you, therefore, brethren, by the mercies of God, that ye present your bodies a living sacrifice, Holy, acceptable into God, which is your reasonable service."

What's consecration? What's the basis of consecration? What is the motive? What is the result of consecration? These are very important questions, and we are going to find the answers, together. What consecration means: the giving of my life to God, to do His will instead of my own. It means, that I present my body as a "living sacrifice."

The animals which were offered to God, in the Old Testament were slain, but they're dead sacrifices. God, doesn't ask me to place my body upon an alter to be slain. Instead, He asked me to become a *"living sacrifice"*, meaning that He wants me to live for Him. Lord, what will thou have me to do?

The sacrifices in the Old Testament, were types of the Lord Jesus. For instance, when a lamb was offered as a sin offering, it was a type or picture of the Lord Jesus dying on the cross, for our sins. But there was another sacrifice which had nothing to do with sin. This sacrifice was called, *"The Burnt Offering."* What did the burnt offering represent? It represents the Lord Jesus offering up, His life, to the Father to do His will. This sacrifice was very precious to God, and from it, we can learn so much about consecration. Consecration, is voluntary. In (Luke 22:42) it says, "Saying, Father, if thou be willing, remove this cup from me, nevertheless not my will, but thine, be done." Concerning "the burnt offering," the Bible says, in (Leviticus 1:2-3) "Speak unto the children of Israel, and say unto them, if any man of you bring an offering unto the Lord, ye shall bring your offering of the cattle, even of the herd, and of the flock." In (Leviticus 1:3) it says, "If His offering be a burnt sacrifice of the herd, let Him offer a male without blemish, he shall offer it of his own voluntary will at the door of the tabernacle of the congregation before the Lord." This, tells us that consecration is unto the Lord, and that it must be voluntary. God doesn't compel me to consecrate my life to Him, instead He says, "I beseech you." God wants me to give my life to Him, not because I have to, but because, I love Him and want to serve Him.

When I consecrated myself to the Lord, did this mean that I'm giving my life to be a preacher, or a missionary? *No*, I *do not* consecrate myself to do, so. I consecrate myself to the Lord, to do His will. Wherever I am, it could be in school, at home or wherever, He may send me. God's the one who decides what He wants me to do and where He wants me to serve Him, and whatever He chooses for me is sure to be the very best for me. **Your Way is Not God's Way**.

Consecration in the offering of a *Whole* life to God. God permitted four kinds of creatures to be used as sacrifices in the burnt offerings. The people who were wealthy brought a costly animal, such as a (bullock), and those with less wealth brought a (sheep), then those who could not afford either of these brought a (dove) or a (pigeon). In each case,it was the offering up, of a whole life to God? God couldn't accept anything, less than this. This, tells us that consecration is the offering up to a *Whole* life to God. I can't give God part of my life and keep part of it to myself. It's not pleasing to God or me. All the joys and blessings in the Christian life depends upon, our holding back, nothing from God.

Consecration is final, once an animal was placed on the altar, as a burnt offering to God, it was not to be taken down. For it, was Holy unto God, the Bible says, in (Leviticus 27:28) "Not withstanding no devoted thing, that a man shall devote unto the Lord of all that He hath, both of man and beast, and of the field of his possession, shall be sold or redeemed: every devoted thing is most Holy unto the Lord."

Once I have dedicated my life to God, I can't take it back, again. God expects my dedication to be a once and for all, giving of myself to Him. Now, what happens if I fall into sin? Does this mean that I "*Must* "rededicate" myself to God? No, it doesn't mean this. If I have sinned, I should confess my sins to God, so that I can once more enjoy His fellowship, but it's not necessary to "rededicate" to God, something that has already been given to Him. Consecration is continual.

"The burnt offering" was offered to God each morning and each evening, day by day, continually. My, consecration began with the act of giving myself to the Lord, but it doesn't end there. I must live out, my consecration. Day by day, I offer myself to the Lord, to do His will instead of my own will.

This is what the Lord Jesus meant, when He said, in (Luke 9:23) "And he said to them all, If any man will come after me, let Him deny himself, and take up his cross daily, and follow me." Why, should I consecrate myself to the Lord? Because, *I Belong To Him.* The Bible says, in (l Corinthians 6:19-20) "What? Know ye not that your body is the temple of the Holy Ghost, which is in you, which ye have of God, and ye are not your own? In, (l Corinthians 6:20) it say, "For ye are bought with a price: therefore Glorify God in your body, and in your spirit, which are God's."

In (Romans 14:8) it says, "And whether we live, we live unto the Lord; and whether we die, we die unto the Lord: whether we life therefore, or die, we are the Lord's." These verses tells me plainly, that I'm not my own, I belong to the Lord. I have been bought with a price. What was the price the Lord Jesus paid for me? With His own precious blood. The Bible says, in (l Peter 1:18-19) "For as much as ye know that ye were not redeemed with corruptible things, as silver and gold, from your vain conversation received by tradition from your fathers." In (l Peter 1:19) it says," But with the precious blood of Christ, as of a lamb without blemish and without spot." Present yourselves unto God, as those that are alive from the dead. The Lord Jesus has redeemed me, He is my Lord and Master, and I belong to Him. Since, I belong to the Lord, it's only right, that I give myself to Him. Consecration is simple, recognizing Christ's ownership, of me and saying to Him, "Lord, I am yours by right, and I wish to be yours by choice."

The Bible makes it very clear, that this is the reasonable service of every born again person. The motive for Consecration, is that I know that I should give myself to the Lord, but what makes me want to do this? It's the love of Christ. The Bible says, in (ll Corinthians 5:14) "For the love of Christ constraineth us; because we thus judge, that if one dead for all, then were all dead." When Christ's love touches my heart, I can do nothing, but fall down before Him and offer my all to Him. So many, of life's little blessing, today, will come unnoticed and slip away, while we continue to grumble and fuss. We ignore God, who gave those blessings to us. How much happier our lives would be if, instead, of complaining, we'd stop and see the numerous blessings, He gives us, each day. Which lighten our burdens and brightens our way.

What's the purpose of Consecration? That God's will, may be done in my life. It's really the Lord Jesus, who does God's will in me. The Bible says, in (Hebrews 13:20-21) "Now the God of peace, that brought again from the dead our Lord Jesus, that great shepherd of the sheep, though the blood of the everlasting covenant." In (Verse 21) it says, "Make you perfect in every good work to do His will, working in you that which is well pleasing in His sight, through Jesus Christ, to whom be Glory for ever and ever." The Gospels, tell us how the Lord Jesus did His Father's will when He lived here on earth. The book of Acts, tell us how He continued to do the Father's will, through the Apostles and Disciples of that day. Now, the Lord Jesus wants to work, through us to do God's will. For this, to happen He needs us to offer our bodies, to Him as a living sacrifice.

The Lord Jesus, doesn't have hands, to do God's, work here on earth, except with our hands. He doesn't have feet to take God's message to the lost except with our feet. No lips, to tell men and women of God's Salvation except with our lips. This is why, the Bible says, in (Romans12:1) "I beseech you therefore, brethren, by the mercies of God, that ye present your bodies a living sacrifice, holy, acceptable unto God, which is your reasonable service." When we give ourselves completely to the Lord Jesus, He will work through us, even as the Father worked through Him.

How do I consecrate myself to God? The Bible tells us, that we're to present ourselves to God. "As those that are alive from the dead." God doesn't want me, to offer my old life to Him. It's the new life, in Christ, which God, wants me to present to Him. The Bible says, in (Romans 6:13) "Neither yield ye your members as instruments of unrighteousness unto sin: but yeild yourselves unto God, as those that are alive from the dead, and your members as instruments of righteousness unto God." God can't use everything from our old life. Only those who are "*alive from the dead*" can serve Him. It's only, as I see that I have been crucified with Christ, buried with Him, and raised up again with Him, that I can truly consecrate my life to God. The result of consecration is, that I die to my own, plans and ambitions, I live, to do the will of God. There again: **Your Way is Not God's Way**.

On this Monday morning, I sit here at my kitchen table, writing and it's a very windy morning. I have all windows open, and the wind chimes in my kitchen are chiming, Oh! The sound is so beautiful. I feel such a joy and unspeakable amount of love and peace. I just want to take the time and say thank you, for your forgiving love and blessings Lord.

The Lord Jesus, is our *Example*. He didn't come into the world to do His own will or to be great in the eyes of men. Oh no! He came to do the will of His Father. Though, He was God, He humbled Himself and took upon Him the form of a servant. He was obedient to the will of God, even unto the death of the cross. God now says, to us in (Philippians 2:5) "Let this mind be in you, which was also in Christ Jesus." Don't think for one minute, that if you, consecrate your life to the Lord, that you will become a world famous preacher or evangelist?

Our Savior, was despised and rejected by men, we're His servants. And the Bible says, in (John 13:16) "Verily, verily, I say unto you, The servant is not greater than his Lord, neither he that is sent greater than he that sent him." *No*, we won't be great in the eyes of men, but there's a great blessing, in consecration finding God's perfect will for our lives.

Our God, has a work for every child of His. The Bible says, in (Ephesians 2:10) "For we are His workmanship, created in Christ Jesus unto good works, which God hath before ordained that we should walk in them." When I consecrate my life to the Lord, He can show me, the works which He has for me. My greatest satisfaction comes, when I find God's will, for my life and do it.

Just think the of joy of meeting the Lord and hearing Him. In (Matthew 25:21) it says, "His Lord said unto him, Well done, thou good and faithful servant: thy hast been faithful over a few things, I will make thee ruler over many things: enter thou into the joy of thy Lord."

God, has asked to me to present my body, to Him as a living sacrifice. There's no substitute for this. Praying, Bible reading, Christian work, witnessing, and going to Church, all these things are good, but they won't take the place of consecration. I hope and pray that you understand, what God, is asking of you.

Do you see, that you belong to Him? And, all that you are and all that you have, for all times. Have you concidered what He has done for you? Has Christ's love touched your heart, so that you can and want to give yourself to Him? If so, here are some Bible verses to carefully read, on consecration. (Romans 8:9-10), (Ephesians 2:10), (Romans 6:13). Let's pray. *"Lord Jesus, this day, I definitely consecrate my life to you, to trust, obey, and serve you the best way I know how, for the rest of my life. I pray that you will enable me to live such a life of faith, love and devotion to you, down here, so it would be pleasing, to you, when I see you, face to face in Heaven. Right here, right now, in your precious name. Thank you, Lord Jesus. Amen and Amen!*

Chapter 14

☙❦❧

In (John 16:13) says, "Howbeit when He, the Spirit of truth, is come, He will guide you into all truth: for He shall not speak of Himself: but whatsoever He shall hear, that shall He speak: and He will shew you things to come." The Holy Spirit, will guide you into all truth. This truth includes, blessings and responsibilities. It's all apart of growing up spiritually. In the natural, a child has only a few responsiblilities. But, as the child matures, he/she should assume more responsibilities. To express their loyalty to Jesus, when He was living on earth. His disciples often called Him, Lord or Master.

Jesus accepted this position, and said, in (John 14:15) "If ye love me, keep my commandments." As a believer, you now belong to Christ. You, use to belong to Satan, but Christ bought you with His blood. When we realize, how much Jesus has done for us. How, He died for us, He saved us from Hell, we are so glad, for opportunities, to show our love for Him by obeying Him. Always put Christ, first in your life.

Cultivate a sense of Christ's presence. Talk to Him in prayer, at definite times, such as mornings, and before going to bed, and throughout the day. When reading your Bible, think of it, as Jesus talking to you. Make Jesus, the center of your life. To mature as a Christian, be sure to attend Church regularly, be around Christian people, for they are positive, in there thinking. Get involved in Church activities. Also, establish a time for private devotions, and for family devotions, if you have a family. All this takes time, but it will be worth it! Give Christ your abilities. Everyone can do something. If you have special talents, dedicate them to the Lord's work. Besides the jobs, which call for special talents, there are many other tasks, where you can help. Your pastor and other Church leaders, will be delighted, to have you volunteer. This helps also, promise the Lord, you will try to do anything, you're asked to do. Everything, you have, is from the Lord. Since, He owns it all anyway, you can really give to Him, by tithing, (giving a tenth of your income to the church), you will help spread the Gospel, at home and in foreign nations. This might sound like a lot, but be assured, that God will meet your needs, as you are faithful to Him. You belong to a new family, (the children of God). Show, you belong to the family, by joining a Bible believing Church. It will give you an increased sense, of belonging and will provide an opportunity to help others. Through, our Church and ministries, we can reach to, the ends of earth. You, also will find your Church ministering to your own needs, too.

Someone, told you about Christ, or you wouldn't be a Christian, today. Christ commanded His Disciples to tell others, in (Matthew 28:18-20) says, "Jesus came and spake unto them, saying, All power is given unto me in Heaven and in earth." In (Verse 19) it says, "Go ye therefore, and teach all nations, baptizing them in the name of the Father, and of the Son, and of the Holy Ghost. In (Verse 20) it says, "Teaching them to observe all things whatsoever I have commanded you: and, lo, I am with you always, even unto the end of the world."

As you witness, at every opportunity, you'll become more effective. Next to your Salvation, your greatest thrill, will be leading someone else to Christ. Talk to someone about God everyday.

In (John 16:7) it says, "Nevertheless I tell you the truth; it is expedient for you that I go away: for if I go not away, the comforter will not come unto you; but if I depart, I will send Him unto you."

In (John 16:33) it says, "These things I have spoken unto you, that in me ye might have peace. In the world ye shall have tribulation: but be of good cheer; I have overcome the world." Also, in (John 17:9) it says, "I pray for them: I pray not for the world, but for them which thou hast given me, for they are thine."

Even before God created the first man, *Adam*, He knew that men would rebel against Him. But God had a great plan. God planned, to call out people from Adam's sinful race and to smite them, into one spiritual body, called the "Church." When you hear the word "Church" you probably think of a building, in which you worship God. One thinks of it's steeple, pulpit, pews, and it's choir loft. But this is only a building, it's not "the Church" that God speaks of in His, Word. The word "Church" as it's used in the New Testament, means, "an assembly of called-out ones." It refers to the *People*, not the building. It's speaking of believers, those whom God has redeemed. The Church, is the "body of Christ." The Church, is more than just a vast number of redeemed people. God, hasn't only called out from Adam's sinful race, a people for His name, but He has united them into one spiritual body, the body of Christ.

Speaking of believers, the Bible says, in (Romans 12:5) "So we, bring many, are one Body in Christ, and every one members one of another." In (Ephesians 5:30, 32) it says, "For we are members of His body, of His flesh, and of His bones." In (Ephesians 5:32) it says, "This is a great mystery: but I speak concerning Christ and the Church." A body must have a head, and Christ is the head of the Church, which is His body.

Speaking of Christ, the Bible says, in (Ephesians 1:22-23) "And hath put all things under His feet, and gave Him to be the head over all things to the Church." In (Ephesians 1:23) it says, "Which is His body, the fullness of Him that filleth all in all." The church was not revealed, in the Old Testament. God's purpose to call people out of Adam's sinful race and unite them into one spiritual body, wasn't revealed to the Old Testament prophets.

But, in the Gospels, (*New Testament*) we find that the Lord Jesus, prayed for His Church before it came to being. In His prayer recorded, in (John chapter 17) "The Lord Jesus prayed not only for the Disciples who were with Him at that time, but also for all who would believe on Him in the future.

In (John 17:20) he said, "Neither pray I for these alone, but for them also which shall believe on me through their word." What did Jesus pray concerning His believers? He prayed that they might be one in "Him." In (John 17:21) it says, "That they all may be one, as thou, Father, art in me, and I in thee, that they also may be one in us, that the world may believe that thou hast sent me." God's answer to this prayer of the Lord Jesus is, "The Church." Why? Because all believers, are made one in the Church, the Body of Christ.

When did the Church come into being? The Church came into being, on the day of Pentecost. The Church, had been in the mind of God from eternity, but it was formed on the day of Pentecost. The word "pente" means "fifty" and the day of Pentecost came exactly fifty days, after the resurrection of the Lord Jesus. The birthday of the Church. Before, He ascended back into Heaven, the Lord Jesus commanded His Disciples to go into the entire world and to preach the Gospel to every creature. But, He also told them to wait for the coming of the Holy Spirit. On the day of Pentecost, 120 Disciples were assembled in an upper room in Jerusalem waiting for the coming of the Holy Spirit. When suddenly, there was a sound from Heaven, like a mighty rushing wind. It filled the house, where, they were sitting. Tongues of fire sat on each of the Disciples. And they, were filled with the Holy Spirit. Something, else happened as the Church was formed. On the day of the Pentecost, the Holy Spirit united the 120 Disciples into one spiritual body, the body of Christ. Through the Holy Spirit, the Disciples were united to each other and to the glorified Lord Jesus, as their head. They had been believers before this time, but now they were the Church, the body of Christ.

The Bible says, in (1 Corinthians 12:13) "For by one spirit are we all baptized into one body, whether we be Jews or Gentiles, whether we be bond or free, and have been all made to drink into one Spirit."

On, that same day, the Gospel was preached to a great multitude of 3,000 and people were saved. The Holy Spirit placed these in the Body of Christ. After this, others were saved daily and added to the Body of Christ. The Bible says, in (Acts 5:14) "And believers were the more added to the Lord, multitudes both of men and women." At first, the Church was composed entirely of Jewish believers, later on, the Gospel was preached to the Gentiles (those who weren't of the Jewish race). Many of them believed, and were added to the body of Christ. In the Church, Jews and Gentiles were made one. Wow! This was a marvelous thing. Why? Because of the hatred and prejudice that existed between the Jews and Gentiles. The Jews, considered the Gentiles, to be unclean and wouldn't even eat with them. The Gentiles likewise despised the Jews. Each considered themselves better than the other. Again, their way, was not God's way. This hatred and prejudice between the Jews and Gentile was a manifestation of "the flesh" that awful sinful nature, which everyone had, both Jews and Gentiles, received from Adam.

How did God deal with this prejudice between them? He, did so by the cross! *All* believers, both Jews and Gentiles were crucified with Christ. Of the Jew and Gentile believers, God made "one man" Jesus Christ the head and all believers forming His spiritual body.

The Bible says, in (Ephesians 2:14-16) "For He is our peace, who hath made both one, and hath broken down the middle wall of petition between us." In (Verse 15) it says, "Having abolished in His flesh the enmity, even the law of commandments, contained in ordinances, for to make in himself of twain one new man, so making peace." In (Verse 16) it says, "And that He might reconcile both unto God in one body by the cross, having slain the enmity, thereby."

In (Colossians 3:11) it says, "Where there is neither Greek nor Jew, circumcision nor uncircumcision, Barbarian, Scythian, bond nor free, but Christ is all, and in all." God has made all believers, one Body of Christ. This is the opposite of what we are by nature. Our life, we all received from Adam, is a life that is, selfish and self centered. This is why we have such a hard time, getting along with other people.

The Apostle Paul, told us what we were like, before God saved us. In (Titus 3:3) it says, "For we ourselves also were sometimes foolish, disobedient, deceived, serving divers lust, and pleasures, living in malice, and envy, hateful, and hating one another."

In (Titus 3:5) it says, "Not by works of righteousness which we have done, but according to His mercy, He saved us, by the washing of regeneration, and renewing of the Holy Ghost." Now, what happened when God saved us? He put us in Christ, on the cross. We were crucified with Him. In Christ, I died to that old life of selfishness and independence. Through my resurrection with Christ, I have become, not only a new creature in Christ, but a member of the Body of Christ. There are 7 mighty bonds of unity.

The Bible tells us that there're 7 mighty bonds, which unite all true believers, those who have been born again of the Spirit of God.

In (Ephesians 4:4-6) it says, "There is one body, and one spirit, even as ye are called in one hope of your calling." In (Verse 5) it says, "One Lord, one faith, one baptism." In (Verse 6) it says, "One God and Father of all, who is above all, and through all, and in you all." Now, let's consider each of these seven bonds of unity.

   1-There's one body. Every person who has received Jesus Christ, as Lord and Savior, is a member of the Body of Christ. Christ has only one body, and all believers are members of His one body. Now, I want you to get this, regardless of the color of a person's skin, regardless of his race, or nationality, or social standing or whether he is rich or poor.If he's a child of God, he's a member of the Body of Christ and one, with those of us, who have been born, again. In (Romans 12:4- 5) it says, "For as we have many members in one body, and all members have not the same office." In (Verse 5) it says, "So we, being many, are one body in Christ, and every one members one of another."

2-There's one Spirit. Every believer has the Holy Spirit dwelling in them because the Holy Spirit is one spirit, He makes us one with all other believers. The Bible says, in (l Corinthians 6:17) it says, "But He that is joined unto the Lord is one Spirit."

3-There's one hope. Every believer has the same hope, the hope of being with the Lord, forever in Glory. This hope is *Certain* because Christ, is living in us by His Spirit. The Bible says, in (Colossians 3:4) "When Christ, who is our life, shall appear, then shall ye also appear with Him in Glory."

4-There's one Lord. The Lord Jesus Christ, all who serve Him are serving the same Lord and are one in Him.

5-There's one faith. True believers may differ, on many matters of scripture interpretation, but there's one faith, which they all have in common, the faith that Jesus Christ, is the Son of God and that He died for their sin and rose again from the grave. This is the faith, that through which every child of God is saved. Glory to His name! The Bible says, in (Galatians 3:26) "For ye are *All* the children of God by faith in Jesus Christ."

6-There's one Baptism. Every believer has been baptized into the body of Christ. This isn't the work of man, but the sovereign work of the Holy Spirit, by which all, who believe in the Savior, are made members of His body. The Bible says, in (l Corinthians 12:13) "For by one spirit are we *All* baptized into one body, whether we be Jews or Gentiles, whether we be bond or free, and have been all made to drink into one Spirit."

7-There's one God and Father. There's only one God, the God and Father of our Lord Jesus Christ, and all who have been born again are members of his family and have the same Heavenly Father. The Church is God's glory. Out of the sinful, self centered race of Adam, God has brought forth the Church, the body of Christ. Through the Church, God is making known His great *Wisdom* and *Power*.

We, now have discovered four great truths about the Church:

1-The Church is the body of Christ.
2-Christ is the *Head* of the body.
3-All believers are members of the body of Christ.
4-The body of Christ is one.

Have we seen God's great plan? Have we realized that we're not, only individual believers, but also members of the body of Christ? Have we seen that all true believers, are members of the same body of Christ? In (Romans 12:5) it says, "So we, being many, are one body in Christ, and every one members on of another." Let's pray, *"Father, help me to see that I'm not only a new creature in Christ, but I'm also a member of the body of Christ. Help me to see that the Body of Christ, is one and that All believers, are members of that, same, one body. In the name of Jesus, I pray. Amen and Amen.*

In (Ephesians 5:32) it says, "This is a great mystery, but I speak concerning Christ and the Church." God has purposed that this "Heavenly Church" the body of Christ, should be expressed here on earth. In each locality, believers are to assemble regularly with other believers for prayer, worship, fellowship, and teaching from God's Word. These assemblies of believers are called "local churches." So, we see, that the Bible uses the word "Church" in two ways:

1- The *Heavenly Church,* which is composed of *All* believers from the day of Pentecost, until the end of this age.
2- The *Local Church,* which is an assembly of believers here on earth. Now, let's see what the Bible says about the first local Churches. One Heavenly Church, the body of Christ.

Many local Churches, Jerusalem, Antioch, Corinth and Ephesus. On the day of Pentecost, there was only one local Church, that, Church was in Jerusalem, later on, we find that there were Churches in many cities. Because of persecution, the believers in Jerusalem were scattered into other cities and nations, where ever they went they preached the Gospel. The apostle Paul was sent on several missionary journey's to preach the Gospel. The Gospel spread and many people believed, and were saved. When a number of people in a city were saved, they became the Church in that city. Thus the Bible speaks of "the Church in Antioch" and "the Church in Corinth" and "the Church in Ephesus."

Each of these local Churches was a true expression of the one Heavenly Church. Christ was the head of each Church and these believers formed His body. Thus in each locality, Christ was able to express His life through the Church in that place.

As the head of the Church, the Lord Jesus gave spiritual gifts to the believers, the members of His body. In each local Church, certain men were recognized as spiritual leaders. These men were called "elders" and they had the spiritual oversight of the Lord's people. So, therefore the Churches were strengthened and increased in number.

The Bible says, in (Acts 16:5) "And so, were the Churches established in the faith, and increased in number daily." So, where did the believers meet? They met, in one another's homes. The place, where they met, wasn't considered to be of great importance, because they knew that the Lord Jesus Himself was there with them. If there's a way, the Lord Jesus will provide it. In (Matthew 18:20) he had promised, "For where two or more are gathered together in my name, there am I in the midst of them."

When did the believers meet? The believers met on the first day of the week, which is Sunday, the

Lord's day. The Bible says, in (Acts 20:7) "And upon the first day of the week, when the Disciples came together to break bread, Paul, preached unto them, ready to depart on the morrow, and continued his speech until midnight."

In, the Old Testament, the Jews were commanded to observe the seventh day, as a Holy day. The New Testament tells us, that as Christians, we're to regard everyday as *Holy*, however, we meet on Sunday, on the last day He rested, we are to rest and keep Holy, the Sabbath.

After you are saved, you need to get into a good Bible teaching Church. Talk to the Lord to help guide you, to the right Church, talk to the Lord, as you would to a friend, for He is the best friend, ever. And don't worry about using the right words. God's more concerned with your attitude, than with your vocabulary. Tell others about what has happened to you.

A witness, is someone who tells others about something, he/she has learned for him/ her self. When you have learned that Jesus can forgive, let others know about it, too. Now for instance, if you take a ember (log) from the fireplace and put it by itself, it will soon go out. In the same way, Christians need the encouragement of other Christians.

Listening to the pastor and other mature Christians preach and teach the Word of God, praying with others, singing together, and making good Christian's fellowship. These things will help you to grow.

In (Hebrews 10:25) it says, "Not forsaking the assembling of ourselves together, as the matter of some is, but exhorting one another, and so much the more, as ye see the day approaching." When God asks you to do something, *Obey* Him. Jesus is your Master, as well as your Savior. Here's a good rule for deciding what is right or wrong. Will this be pleasing to God? Make this the ruling factor in all you do or say. Spiritual maturity doesn't depend on how long, you have been saved. If you follow these simple steps, you will begin to become a mature Christian, one who pleases God, and one He can use.

In (John 5:39) it says, "Search the scriptures, for in them ye think ye have eternal life, and they are they which testify of me." In (John 4:24) it says, "God is a Spirit, and they that worship Him, must worship Him in Spirit and in Truth."

The Lord Jesus gave His Church two ordinances:

1-Baptism.
2-The Lord's Supper.

We observe these same two ordinances, today. But, first what is an ordinance? An ordinance, is a ceremony, ordained by Christ which pictures a spiritual truth. Sometimes, we can see and feel, which symbolizes a spiritual truth.

What is Baptism? Baptism, is a ceremony, which pictures our union, with Christ in His death, burial, and resurrection. When we stand in the water, to be baptized we testify to the fact, that we have been crucified with Christ, when we are placed under the water, we picture our burial with Him, and when we are lifted up out of the water, we picture our resurrection with Him.

In (Romans 6:4) it says, "Therefore we are buried with Him by baptism into death, that like as Christ was raised up from the dead by the glory of the Father, even so, we also should walk in newness of life." The Lord Jesus, commanded every one, who believes in Him to be baptized. By baptism, we give public testimony, to the fact, that we are united with Him in His death, burial and resurrection, personally identified with Christ. 1-Crucified with Him. 2-Buried with Him. 3-Risen with Him.

What's the Lord's Supper? The Lord's Supper, is a time of remembrance, of our Saviors death on the cross. The cup which we drink, represents His blood, which was shed for our sins. The bread, of which we partake, represents His body which was broken for us. The Bible says, we are to observe the Lord's Supper till Jesus comes again.

In (l Corinthians 11:24) it says, "And when He had given thanks, He brake it, and said, "Take, eat, this is my body, which is broken for you, this do in remembrance of me." Also, in (Verse 25) it says, "After the same manner also He took the cup, when He had supped, saying, This cup is the new testament in my blood, this do ye, as oft as ye drink it, in remembrance of me". And, in (Verse 26) it says, "For as often as ye eat this bread, and drink this cup, ye do shew the Lord's death till He come." Now, let's look at another great truth which concerns all believers. All believers are "priests unto God."

In the Old Testament, we find that there were men, who were called of God, to be priests. The priests had access to God and they served God. It was a great honor to be a priest, but only the men of one tribe. The tribe of Levi, could be priests. Those, who weren't priests couldn't approach God directly, they couldn't make sacrifices to God, directly, and they couldn't serve God, directly. Everything, had to be done for them, by the priests, even the priests themselves, had to have a high priest, and he alone, could enter the most Holy place where the Glory of God, dwelt. We see that the children of Israel, were divided into two classes:

1-The people of God.
2-The priests of God.

In the New Testament, we find that All believers, are people unto God. There's isn't any special class among the people of God. In (Matthew 23:8, 9) it says, "But be not ye called Rabbi, for one is your master, even Christ, and all ye are brethren." In (Verse 9) it says, "And called no man your father upon the earth, for one is your Father, which is in Heaven." Twice in the New Testament, we find that the whole body of Christians, all believers, are declared to be priests.

The Bible says, in (l Peter 2:5,9) it says, "Ye also, as lively stones, are built up a spiritual house, an holy priesthood, to offer up spiritual sacrifices, acceptable to God by Jesus Christ." In (Verse 9) it says, "But ye are a chosen generation, a royal priesthood, an holy nation, a peculiar people, that ye should shew forth the praises of Him who hath called you out of darkness into His marvelous light."

In the New Testament *Every* believer, is a priest unto God. Now, what does it mean, when we say that every believer is a "Priest unto God?" First, it means, that we can come directly to God. We doen't need a priest, to talk to God for, us. Why? Because every believer is a priest. The Lord Jesus, is our great high priest, through Him *Only*, we confess our sins, directly to God and receive forgiveness, directly from God.

The Bible says, in (l Timothy 2:5) "For there is one God, and one mediator between God and men, the man Jesus Christ." Second, it means, that all believers should serve God. The Lord Jesus, Himself has chosen us and ordained us to serve Him.

He said, in (John 15:16) "Ye have not chosen me, but I have chosen you, and ordained you, that ye should go and bring forth fruit, and that your fruit should remain, that whatsoever ye shall ask of the Father in my name, He may give it you."

Our first responsibility, as Christians, is to *Love, Obey*, and *Serve* the Lord Jesus. Every believer, should worship the Lord, a Bible student, a soul winner, one who serves the Lord Jesus Christ.

Now, let's consider, how does the Church function? It, functions as a *Living Body*. The Church isn't simply a organization, it's the living body of Christ, and it must function as a body.

Writing to the believers in Corinth, the Apostle Paul says, in (l Corinthians 12:27) "Now ye are the body of Christ, and members in particular." What, was Paul saying to these believers? He was saying, you are the body of Christ in Corinth. Christ is the head and you are His body, through which He expresses His life in the city of Corinth. You must recognize this great truth, that you are Christ's body and you must work together, as the body of Christ.

What was true of the Church in Corinth, should be true of every local Church, today and forever. The local Church, in a city, should function as a living body.

In (Ephesians 5:30) it says, "For we are members of His body, of His flesh, and of His bones." There are 4 great facts, concerning how a body functions and these things are true of our human body, and true also of Christ's, body.

- 1-The body has many different parts and all are needed. In our human body, we have many different parts, eyes, ears, mouth, nose, fingers, hands, feet and legs, etc. All are different, yet all are needed. Christ's body has many members, also.

In, the Bible (1 Corinthians 12:14, 21) it says, "For the body is not one member, but many." In (Verse 21) it says, "And the eye can not say unto the hand, I have no need of thee, nor again the head to the feet, I have no need of you."

- 2-Every member must function. If my eyes are not seeing, I can't see, if my ears are not hearing, I can't hear, if my legs are not working, I can't walk. When a member of the body, doesn't function, the whole body suffers a loss. Therefore, Christ's body is handicapped, when a member of His body, isn't functioning.

Every believer, is a member of Christ's body and every believer has at least one gift of the Spirit. Meaning, as a believer, you have a special ability that is needed by the body of Christ. Each believer should say, "Lord, where do I serve in your body, of the Church?" What, is it that you want me to do?

The Bible says, that the Body of Christ is built, up in love, by that which *Every Believer* supplies.

3-All members must obey the head. In order for my body, to function properly, all the members must obey the head. This is true of Christ's body, also.

The Bible says, that we are to "hold fast the head." This, means that we are to obey Christ. In (Ephesians 5:23,24) it says, "For the husband is the head of the wife, even as Christ is the head of the Church, and He is the savior of the body." In (Verse 24) it says, "Therefore as the Church is subject unto Christ, so let the wives be to their own husbands in everything." If we are subject unto Christ, we'll be subject to God's Word. We'll also be in submission to those whom God, has placed in positions of leadership in the Church. In (Hebrews 13:17) it says, "Obey them that have the rule over you, and submit yourselves, for they watch for your souls, as they that must give account, that they may do it with joy, and not with grief, for that is unprofitable for you."

4-All members must work together. God wants a body, not a lot of sinless, isolated Christians. The Bible says, we are "One body in Christ." Alone, I can't serve God effectively. We must work together with other members of Christ's, body. Some, Christians look at the imperfections, in the Church and decide that they don't need the Church. This is a very serious mistake. The Church isn't perfect, it's made up of imperfect people, such as you and I, but it's Gods chosen vessel, to express the life of His Son here on earth. When the Church assembles, every member of the body of Christ, has God given, responsibility to attend and participate. This includes our children, young people, and adults. Each member must answer to the Lord, for his/ her failure to do, this.

The Bible tells us that, in the last days, men shall be lovers of pleasure more that lovers of God. Sad, but true! How is it, when Gods people allow the fleeting pleasures of this world, to draw them away from their place in the Church? The body of Christ, not only needs us, but we need the body. We can't be strong Christians, unless we share in the life of the body. When we meet with the other members of Christ body, we receive strength and life from the body. By God's grace, we must see that we're a member, of the body of Christ, in the place where we live.

When the body assembles, we must be there and participate, this isn't only a great responsibility, but one which we shouldn't take lightly. Many Christians don't have the privilege of freely meeting together. So, don't neglect the Church.

In the Bible it says, (Hebrews 10:25) "Not forsaking the assembly of ourselves together, as the manner of some is, but exhorting one another, and so much the more, as ye see the day approaching." So remember, I'm a member of the body of Christ. (The body needs me, and I need the body.)

Chapter 15

❦

In the midst of Satan's evil world system, Christ has a body though which He can work and manifest His mighty, victorious power. It's through the Church that Christ expresses His life and does His work in the world. We, are going to consider the mission of the Church, what the Church is supposed to do. The mission of the Church, is to proclaim the Gospel, to every person in the world. Every believer has a part in this.

The Lord Jesus said, in (Mark 16:15) "And He said unto them, Go ye into all the world, and preach the Gospel to every creature." It has been nearly 2,000 years, since our Lord gave this command to his Disciples, yet today there are still millions of people who are unsaved. These unsaved people can be divided into two groups:

1- Those that have heard the Gospel but rejected it.
2- Those who have never heard of the Gospel.

We're going to be thinking about the second group, those who have *Not* heard the Gospel, and have no true knowledge of God. We want to see what their spiritual condition is and what God has told us to do about it. One thing is for sure, they are in total spiritual darkness and under the power of Satan. How do we know this? Because they commit terrible sins, they worship idols of wood and stones. They live in fear of evil spirits,and they are afraid to die.

In some countries, mothers throw their babies to crocodiles, others cut themselves and walk on beds of spikes. Why do they do these things? Because, they have been told that by doing these things, their sins will be forgiven.

In other countries, people are highly civilized, yet they don't know God. They may not worship idols of wood and stone, nevertheless, they too, are in spiritual darkness and under the power of Satan.

The Bible, describes them as being "without Christ" having no hope, and without God.

Of course, those in Christian lands, who have rejected the Gospel, are no better off than those who have never heard the Gospel. Indeed, they will be judged more severely by God, because they rejected the Gospel.

Did God create people with no knowledge of himself? No, he didn't. Man, was created (Putz) in the image of God, but man turned away from God.

In the first chapter of Romans, we read about mans downward steps away from God. When they knew God, they didn't glorify Him as God, nor were they thankful. They became foolish in their imaginations and had hearts that were darkened. Claiming to be wise, they became fools. Instead, of worshipping the glorious God, who created them, they made images of birds, beasts, and snakes and worshipped these, idols. After this, they went into terrible wickedness and immorality. These men went from spiritual light, into spiritual darkness.

We read, in (Romans 1:21-32) "Because that, when they knew God, they glorified Him, not as God, neither were thankful, but because vain in their imaginations, and their foolish heart was darkened." In (Verse 22) it says, "Professing themselves to be wise, they become fools." In (Verse23) it says, "And changed the glory of the incorruptible God into an image made like to corruptible man, and to birds, and four footed beasts, and creeping things." In(Verse 24) it says, "Wherefore God also gave them up to uncleanness through the lust of their own hearts, to dishonor their own bodies between themselves." In (Verse 25) it says, "Who changed the truth of God into a lie, and worshipped and served the creature more than the Creator, who is blessed for ever. In (Verse 26) it says, "For this cause God gave them up unto vile affections, for even their women did change the natural use into that which is against nature." In (Verse 27) it says, "And likewise also the men, leaving the natural use of the women, burned in their lust one toward another, men with men working that which is unseemly, and receiving in themselves that recompense of their error which was meet." In (Verse 28) it says, "And even as they did not like to retain God in their knowledge, God gave them over to a reprobate mind, to do those things which are not convenient." In(Verse 29) it say, "Being filled with all unrighteousness, fornication, wickedness, covetousness, maliciousness, full of envy, murder, debate, deceit, malignity, whisperers." In (Verse 30) it says, "Backbiters, haters of God, despiteful, proud, boasters, inventors of evil things, disobedient to parents." In(Verse 31) it says, "Without understanding, covenant breakers, without natural affection, implacable, unmerciful." In (Verse 32) it says, "Who knowing the judgment of God, that they which commit such things are worthy of death, not only do the same, but have pleasures in them that do them." Man's downward steps away from God.

Are those who have never heard the Gospel lost? Yes, they are lost. Every person without Christ, is lost. Those who die in their sins will be forever separated from God, in the lake of fire.

The Bible says, in (Psalms 9:17) "The wicked shall be turned into Hell, and all the nations that forgot God." If you're not saved, it's never too late, to ask Christ into your life. Do, it right, now! Don't wait. God loves you, and wants you to come home to be with Him.

Why, are those who have not heard the Gospel lost? They are lost for two reasons:

1-They are sinners.
2-They don't know Christ as their Savior.

Although, these people don't have God's Word, they know that they do, wrong things. How do they know? Because, God has put His laws into their hearts and consciences. They know that lying, stealing, murder, adultery, and the other things they do wrong, yet they do these things, anyway. So, therefore they're sinners and they'll be judged for their sins.

The Bible says, in (Ezekiel 18:4) "Behold, all souls are mine, as the soul of the Father, so also the soul of the son is mine, the soul that sinneth, it shall die."

Can their religions save them? Many people believe that if these people are sincere in their religions, God will somehow, save them. Is this true? No, it's not. The Bible, makes it very clear, that a person can't be saved unless he personally receives the Lord Jesus Christ as his Savior. Christ is our Savior.

The Lord Jesus, said in (John 14:6) "Jesus saith unto him, I am the way, the truth, and the life, no man cometh unto the Father, but by me."

Salvation, is in Christ and in Him, alone. In (Acts 4:12) says, "Neither is there Salvation in any other, for there is none other name under Heaven given among men, whereby we must be saved."

Those who, worship idols may be sincere in their religions, but their worship isn't acceptable to God.

The Bible says, that when people sacrifice to idols, they are actually worshipping Satan and his evil spirits. You can see from this, why God hates *All* false religions, and why He won't accept those who worship idols.

Can these people be saved? Yes, of course! The Gospel is for all men. The Bible says, that the Gospel of Christ "is the power of God unto salvation to *Every*

One that believeth." The Gospel of Jesus Christ turns men from darkness to, light.

Four important questions. The Bible says, "Whosoever shall call upon the name of the Lord shall be saved." But the Bible, asks these questions, about those who haven't heard the Gospel:

1- How can they call on Christ, if they do believed in Him?
2- How can they believe in Him, if they have not heard the Word?
3- How can they hear about Him without a preacher?
4- How can a preacher, preach to them unless he is sent?

In (Romans 10:14-15) it says, "How then shall they call on Him in whom they have not, believed? And, how shall they believe in Him of whom they have not heard? And, how shall they hear without a preacher?" In (Verse 15) it says, "And how shall they preach, except they be sent? As it is written, how beautiful are the feet of them that preach the Gospel of peace, and bring glad tidings of good things!" Can people call on the Lord Jesus, if they don't believe in Him? No, they can't.

Can they believe in Him, if they have never heard of Him? No, they can't. Can they hear of Him, unless someone tells them? No, they can't. Therefore, someone must go, and tell them about the Lord Jesus, so they can be saved.

Who will tell them about Jesus? Those who have been saved. The Bible says, in (ll Corinthians 5:18) "And all things are of God, who hath reconciled us to Himself by Jesus Christ, and hath given to us the ministry of reconciliation."

The great commission is our Lord's command to His disciples to, go into all the world and to preach the Gospel to every creature. In (Mark 16:15) it says, "And He said unto them, Go ye unto all the world, and preach the Gospel to every creature." Has the great Commission been fulfilled? No, it hasn't.

Millions of people are still in spiritual darkness and under the power of Satan. Most of the people in the world, have never seen a Bible, and never heard the name of Jesus. They're without Christ and without hope.

The words of a pagan woman should stir our hearts. She said, "Tell your people how fast we are dying. Ask them if they can send the Gospel a little faster." The whole world must hear the Gospel. The Lord Jesus has commanded us to preach the Gospel to every creature. We, must obey Him. If we don't do what we can, to take the Gospel to the lost, God will hold us responsible.

He said, in (Ezekiel 3:18) "When I say unto the wicked, thou shalt surely die, and thy giveth him not warning, nor speakest to warn the wicked from his wicked way, to save his life, the same wicked man shall die in his iniquity, but His blood will I require at thine hand." We can't close our eyes, to the terrible condition of the lost and escape our, responsibility. Every Christian must, one day, stand before the

Judgment seat of Christ, to give an account of his life, after he was saved.

If we fail, to do what, we can do, to send the Gospel to every person, we'll have to answer to the Lord for our neglect. We can't say that we didn't know about their needs.

The Lord Jesus said, in (John 4:35) "Say not ye, There are yet four months, and then cometh harvest? Behold, I say unto you, lift up your eyes, and look on the fields, for they are white already to harvest." What can we do? If those who haven't heard the Gospel, are to have a chance to be saved, every believer, must do all he can, under God's direction, to get the Gospel to them. God has a work for every Christian, in fulfilling the great commission.

Here are five things we all can do:

1-Witness God's plan for evangelizing. The Word is for everyone, who knows the story of Jesus, to tell it to someone else, not only with his lips, but also with his life. The Lord Jesus said, "Ye shall be witnesses unto me." Begin right now, being a witness for the Lord Jesus, right where you are.
2-Pray. We can pray that God will send forth missionaries to the unsaved, and we can pray daily for the missionaries God has already sent forth. The Lord Jesus said, in (Luke 10:2) "Therefor said unto them, The harvest truly is great, but the laborers are few, pray ye therefore the Lord of the harvests, that he would send forth laborers into his harvest."

3-Give. When we give money to the Lord's work, we're sharing in that work, and we'll share in the rewards one day. We should give wisely, seeing to it, that our money goes to those who are faithfully preaching the Gospel. We should give joyfully knowing that our money is being used, so that others may have eternal life.

4-Prepare. If we want to be useful servants of the Lord, we must prepare ourselves. We can do this by setting aside time, each day for Bible study and prayer, by memorizing scriptures. Get your tools ready, and God will use you!

5-Go. We don't need to ask the Lord *If* He wants us to serve Him. God calls all of His children to serve Him. The only question you and I must ask is, "Lord, where will you have me to, go?"

We have learned something, of the terrible condition, of those who don't know God. We have learned of our responsibility, as a Christian to get the Gospel to them.

Now, the question is, *What Will You Do?* Will you be, a faithful witness for the Lord Jesus, where you are? Will you pray, that God will send forth laborers into the harvest field? Will you give, so that others may hear God's Word? Will you prepare yourself to serve the Lord more effectively? Will you go where God calls you to go?

Remember this, "We only have one life, it soon will past. Only, what is done for Christ will last."

Who is going to take the Gospel to the world? Those who are servants of God. We, who are saved, are called to serve God, and take the Gospel to the lost. We must not forget, that we ourselves, were once lost, dead in trespasses and sins, and separated from the life of God.

A servant of God, told us about the Lord Jesus, we believed on Him, and became children of God, through faith in Jesus Christ. Now, we must become servants of God, that others may hear the Gospel and be saved.

Sinner- Son-Servant! These are the vial links in God's plan for getting the Gospel to the world.

Sinners will hear the Gospel, believe on the Lord Jesus, and become His children. In time, they become servants to God and take the Gospel to others.

We're going to learn how we can begin preparing ourselves to be effective servants of God. To become a doctor, teacher, or lawyer, one must spend many, many hours preparing themselves for that profession.

To become an effective servant of God also requires diligent preparation. The Bible says, in (ll Timothy 2:15) "Study to shew thy self approved unto God, a workman that needeth not to be ashamed, rightly dividing the Word of truth.

To be an effective servant of God two things are absolutely essential:

1-A working knowledge of the Bible.
2-Daily fellowship with the Lord Jesus.

Now, how do we obtain, a working knowledge of the Bible? By reading it and studying it, and by memorizing portions of the Bible.

The Bible is the most important book, in all the world, yet, it's very sad to say, "many Christians don't take the time to read it and become familiar with it."

As, we read the Bible, we must depend upon the Holy Spirit, to reveal it's truth to us. The Bible is different from other books, it can't be understood, without the illumination of the Holy Spirit. This explains why an unsaved person can't understand the Bible. He doesn't understand the Bible, because he doesn't have the Holy Spirit. The Bible says, in (l Corinthians 2:14) "But the natural man (the unsaved man) receiveth not the things of the Spirit of God, for they are foolishness unto Him, neither can He know them, because they are spiritually discerned." Those who have been born again, have the Holy Spirit dwelling in them, therefore they can understand the things of God.

The Bible says, in (l Corinthians 2:12) "Now, we have received, not the spirit of the world, but the Spirit which is of God, that we might know the things that are freely given to us of God."

Every time we open God's Word to read it, let's pause for a moment, to pray and ask God and the Holy Spirit to reveal it's truths to us.

David's prayer is a good one for us. In (Psalms 119:18) "Open thou mine eyes, that I may behold wondrous things out of thy law."

The Bible contains:

1-Facts to be believed.
2-Promises to be claimed.
3-Commands to be obeyed.
4-We grow by obeying God's Word.

Christians should grow in grace and in knowledge, of the Lord Jesus Christ. To grow, we must have spiritual food. Now, what *is* our spiritual food? Our spiritual food is the <u>WORD</u> <u>OF</u> <u>GOD</u>.

The Bible says, in (l Peter 2:2) "As newborn babes, desire the sincere milk of the Word, that ye may grow thereby." When we eat, we take food into our bodies, it becomes a part of us. We must likewise, take God's Word into our lives, it must also, become a part of us. How do we take God's Word into our lives? By obeying it!

The Bible says, in (James 1:22) "Be ye doers of the Word, and not hearers only, deceiving your own selves." As we read God's Word, let's believe it's truths, claim it's promises, and obey it's commands. Let's begin today!

Begin reading God's Word today. Start with the Gospel of John. Ask the Holy Spirit to help you understand it, then mark the verses that seem to speak especially to your heart. This will make your Bible even more valuable to you. I have learned that a colored pencil is best for this. (Do *not* use a ball point ink pen, because it will bleed through the pages of most Bibles.)

In the Gospel of John, you'll find that Jesus *is* the, Word of God. He *is* the Lamb of God. He *is* the living bread which came down from Heaven. He *is* the way, the truth, and the life. He *is* the good shepherd. He *is* the resurrection and the life. He *is* the true vine. He *is* the one who died for our sins and He *is* the living resurrected Christ.

After you have read the Gospel of John, read the book of Acts. This book, will tell about the early days of the Church. Then, begin with Matthew and read the entire New Testament, and finally, read the Old Testament. This will take a lot of time, but it will be time well, spent.

One thing I have learned, as you read the Bible, don't be unduly concerned, about things that you don't fully understand. I've always said, "*that reading the Bible is like eating fish.* When you are eating fish, you may come across a bone occasionally. What, do you do, when you come across a bone? You simply lay it aside, and keep on eating the yummy, fish. You don't throw the fish away, just because you find a bone. Likewise, when you come across something in the Bible, that you don't understand, just think there's a bone, something I don't understand. I will lay it aside for now, and keep on reading God's Word."

Remember this, don't allow your *Faith,* to be shaken by those who claim to find errors and contradictions, in the Bible. For hundreds of years unbelieving man, tried to discredit the Bible, yet it still stands today as the infallible Word of God. The quickest and most effective way to gain a understanding of the Bible, is to memorize portions of it.

So, often we have wanted to witness to others, but we didn't know what to say. If you have memorized scriptures, you can boldly say here's what God says, in the Bible and you can say it with confidence because, it's the Word of God.

Always, remember that it's not our words, but the Word of God, which the Holy Spirit uses, in the Salvation of others.

The Bible says, in (l Peter 1:23) "Being born again, not of corruptible seed, but of incorruptible, by the Word of God, which liveth and abideth forever."

Get your tools ready and God will use you. Every time you memorize a portion of God's Word, you're equipping yourself with another tool to use in serving God. The real secret of memorizing is, *Repetition.* If you say, something over and over enough times, you will memorize it. The best and simplest way to memorize a verse is through the use of cards. Purchase some 3x5 index cards, on one side of a card, write the verse you want to learn, on the other side write the reference. Now, be sure to copy the verses correctly. Carry the cards with you and go through them, as often as you can. Look at the reference, on each card and see if you can quote the verse, then check yourself by turning the card over and reading it, correctly. Do this over and over, again. Don't be satisfied until you can quote the verses perfectly. Soon, you'll find that you have memorized those verses, and then you can add more verses. You will feel so good about, yourself. You can add verses each week, but make sure to review the ones you have already learned. Review! Review! Review! You can memorize scriptures. Don't, excuse yourself by saying, "that you have a poor memory," until you have honestly tried these, simple tools. The verses you memorize are the tools you'll use as the servant of God. Here's a few verses, to get you started:

<u>First week</u>: Romans 3:23, Romans 6:23, John 3:16, John 1:12 and John 3:36.
<u>Second week</u>: Romans 3:10, Hebrews 9:27, Romans 5:8, Acts 16:31 and l John 5:11-12
<u>Third week</u>: Isaiah 53: 5-6, l Peter 3:18, John 14:6, Acts 4:12 and John 3:3.
<u>Fourth week</u>: Titus 3:5, Ephesians 2: 8-9, Galatians 3:26, Galatians 4:6, and l John 5:13

These verses are short and very easy to memorize.

A dictionary is the only place where "success" comes before "work"

If you, want to become an effective servant of God, you must not only have a working knowledge of the Bible, but you must also have daily fellowship, with the Lord Jesus.

The secret of a strong Christian life, is to have a daily quiet-time. What is quite time? It's a time spent alone with the Lord, each day in the studying of His Word and in prayer. So, many wonderful blessings will come to us, if we establish a quiet time and keep it faithfully.

1- We'll become more like Christ. It's by beholding the Glory of the Lord Jesus, that we're made like Him, of course, we can't see Jesus in person at this time. But, we can behold His Glory by reading about Him in our Bibles.

The Bible is like a mirror; by reading it, we'll see Jesus.

The Bible says, in (ll Corinthians 3:18) "But we all, with open face beholding as in a glass the Glory of the Lord, are changed into the same image from Glory to Glory, even as by the Spirit of the Lord."

2-God reveals His will to us. Usually, it's when we're alone with the Lord, that He speaks to us through His Word and reveals His will, to us.

For me, the Lord speaks to me, in the very early morning hours, there's something about those early morning hours, that the Lord, so clearly speaks to my heart. He speaks to me in a soft quiet voice, He never yells, I can feel His presence. This is the greatest blessing of all. There's no other way to get to know God. We, must spend time alone with God to know Him, and to become conscious of His presence and to be filled with His power, God said, in (Psalms 46:10) "Be still, and know that I am God, I will be exalted among the heathen, I will be exalted in the earth." To establish a quiet time, three things are necessary, a definite place, time and a plan:

1-Find a place where you can be alone with the Lord. A place with good lighting and a table where you can lay your books and write notes.
2-Decide on a definite time. For most people, the best time is first thing in the morning. For myself, this is so very true. Great musicians

always tune their instruments before a concert, not after it. It's much better for us to meet with the Lord, first thing in the morning and with our *Hot Coffee*, then come to Him, at the end of the day, with a long list of failures to, confess.

The importance of spending the first hour, of each day with the Lord can't be over emphasized. The Bible says, of the Lord Jesus, "And in the morning, rising up a great while before day, He went out and departed into a solitary place, and there prayed." If the sinless, Lord Jesus, found it necessary to spend time alone with His Father each day, how much more should, we. Since, we're serious about preparing ourselves to serve God. This is one practical way in which you can show the Lord, how much you love Him.

3-Have a definite plan. Begin your quiet time with a short prayer, to the Lord, asking Him to speak to your heart through His Word. Then open the Bible and begin reading. Don't be in a hurry, take your time to think about what you are reading. Sometimes, you have to read it several times, for the message to sink in. Talk to God about what you are reading. Often, a particular verse will be especially, meaningful to you. Write it down on a card and memorize it.

Now, how much time should I spend with God? This is up to you. A half an hour is minimum, an hour is whole lot better. Remember there's 24 hours in each day, and every serious minded Christian should be able to set aside one of these hours for, God.

Spend the first part of your time, reading the Bible, then turn to the Lord in prayer. Confess your sins to Him. Praise Him for all that He means to you. Thank Him for His wonderful blessings. Pray for those whom He brings to your mind. Ask for His guidance throughout the day. Tell Him that you love Him. Once, you have established your place, time and plan, *Stick to it*. If you allow everything that comes along, to disrupt your quite time, soon you won't have *any* quite time at, all. Don't excuse yourself by saying, "I don't have time." It's true, that we don't have time to do everything, that we want to do, but, we must choose the things are most important. We must put first things first.

Jesus said, in (Matthew 6:33) "But seek ye first the Kingdom of God, and His righteousness, and all these things shall be added unto you." Let me say this, "be prepared for all kinds of opposition to your establishing your quiet time. Satan, knows what a daily quiet time does, in bringing power into the life of a child of God, and he'll do all he can to prevent, you from establishing this, great habit in your life."

There's a price to pay in becoming an effective servant of God, you must spend time learning God's Word. You, must spend time memorizing scripture verses. The best of all, it's spending time with the Lord. There's no need in talking about, how much you love the Lord and how much you want to serve Him, if you don't have time for Him and for His

Word. God isn't impressed with our words, He looks at our actions. In (l Samuel 2:3) it says, "Talk no more so exceeding proudly, let not arrogancy come out of your mouth, for the Lord is a God of knowledge, and by Him actions are weighed."

Do, you want to know the key to success for a Christian? It's simply this, *Put God First*. God says, in (l Samuel 2:30) "Wherefore the Lord God of Israel saith, I said indeed that thy house, and the house of thy Father, should walk before me for ever, but now the Lord saith, be it far from me, for them that honor me I will honor, and they that despise me shall be lightly esteemed."

Do you want your life to count for God? Then, begin reading God's Word daily. Start memorizing scriptures. Establish your quiet time and keep it faithfully. Begin right now!!

Go to God in prayer each day.
Read God's Word every day.
Obey God in all things.
Witness for Christ each day.

Chapter 16

Every Christian, is called upon, to witness for Christ and every Christian can be a soul-winner.

The Lord Jesus said, in (Matthew 4:19) "And He saith unto them, Follow me, and I will make you fishers of men." Why, is it so important to learn how to win others to Christ? Why is the human soul such a great value? It will live forever. Every person you meet has a soul, that will live forever, either in the blessings of Heaven or in the miseries of hell. The Bible says, in (John 3:36) "He that believeth on the Son hath everlasting life, and he that believeth not the Son shall not see life, but the wrath of God abideth on him."

God values the souls of us all, so highly that He sent His Son to die on the cross, that we all might be saved. When we see how precious we all are to God, we'll do all we can to win them to Christ.

Every human soul will live forever, in one of two places! Heaven or Hell.

We, must use God's Word to win souls, we must know how to use the Word of God. Just as a doctor don't give the same prescription to every patient, so the same verse won't meet the need of every person. You must have a good working knowledge of the Bible. We, must have *God's Power*, if we're to be soul winners, we also need something, else. The soul winner's power, that comes from the Holy Spirit.

When the Lord Jesus, commanded His Disciples to preach the Gospel to every creature, He also promised them the power of the Holy Spirit.

He said, in (Acts 1:8) "But ye shall receive power, after that the Holy Ghost is come upon you, and ye shall be witnesses unto me both in Jerusalem, and in all Judaea, and in Samaria, and unto the uttermost part of the earth." On, the day of Pentecost, the Disciples were filled with the Holy Spirit. Peter stood up and preached, in the power of the Holy Spirit and approximately 3,000 souls were saved. Today, every believer has the Holy Spirit dwelling in them.

It's the Holy Spirit who convicts people of sin, it's the Holy Spirit, who shows people their need of a Savior and it's the Holy Spirit who reveals Christ to them.

Ask God to fill you, with the Holy Spirit so that you can be an effective soul-winner. The soul-winner's message is the Gospel. The word "Gospel" means "good news." And, the good news is that Christ died for our sins and rose again to be our living Savior.

The Apostle Paul, wrote in (l Corinthians 15:1,3-4) "Moreover, brethren, I declare unto you the Gospel which I preached unto you, which also ye hath received, and wherein ye stand." In (Verse 3) it says, "For I delivered unto you first of all that which I also received, how that Christ died for our sins according to the scriptures." In (Verse 4) it says, "And that He was buried, and that He rose again the third day according to scriptures."

There are four basic truths, in the Gospel's message:

1-The fact of sin.
2-The penalty of sin.
3-Christ paid the penalty.
4-We must receive Christ.

Get these four facts firmly fixed in your mind, because you'll use them in leading souls to Christ. In leading someone to Christ, you simply explain the four basic truths of the Gospel. In (Romans 3:23) it says, "For all have sinned, and come short of the Glory of God."

1-Leading a person to Christ, to show him, with God's Word that He's a sinner. A good passage of scriptures for this is found, in (Romans 3:10-12) "As it is written, THERE IS NONE RIGHTEOUS, NO, NOT ONE." In (Verse 11) it says, "THERE IS NONE THAT UNDERSTANDETH, THERE IS NONE THAT SEEKETH AFTER GOD." In (Verse 12) it says, "THEY ARE ALL GONE OUT OF THE WAY, THEY ARE TOGETHER BECOME UNPROFITABLE, THERE IS NONE THAT DOETH GOOD, NO, NOT ONE." This is what God says, about us. Before a person can be saved, he must realize that he's a sinner and is willing to give up his sins.

2-The Lord Jesus said, in (Luke 13:5) it says, "I tell you, nay, but, except ye repent, ye shall all likewise perish." In (Romans 6:23) it says, "For the wages of sin is death, but the gift of God is eternal life through Jesus Christ our Lord."

Explain the word "death" as used here, means separation from God, in the lake of fire, forever. Because, we're sinners and condemned to eternal death, we need a Savior.

3-The next verse is a very familiar one, found in (John 3:16) it says, "For God so loved the world, that He gave His only begotten Son, that whosoever believeth in Him should not perish, but have everlasting life."

Whom does God mean when He says "the world"? He means everyone. This includes you and I. What did God give to us? He gave His Son to us. Meaning that He, gave us Jesus to die on the cross for our sins. Why did God give us a Savior? He loves us and we *Need* a Savior. We, can't save ourselves, so God gave us Jesus, to be our, Savior.

If I give you something, do you have to pay for it? No! Do you have to work for it? No! But there's one thing you must do, you must receive it. God has given the Lord Jesus, to us to be our Savior, but we must receive Him.

4-In (John 1:12) it says, "But as many as received Him, to them gave He power to become the sons of God, even to them that believe on His name." How, does one become a child of God? By receiving the Lord Jesus.

Now you can ask these questions, do you believe that Jesus Christ is the Son of God? Do you believe that He died on the cross for our sins and rose again? Do you believe that He is *able* to save you? Do you believe that He will, come into your heart and save you right, now, if you asked Him to? If, the answer is *yes* to all of these questions. Would you like to ask the Lord Jesus, to come into your heart, right now?

If so, then right here right now, let's pray this prayer. *"Lord Jesus, I know that I am a sinner, I believe that you are the Son of God, and that you died on the cross for my sins. Forgive me Lord, for all of my sins right here, right now, please come into my heart and be my Savior. Your will be done, in your Holy Name, we pray. Thank you, Lord and I receive you right now. Amen.*

When a person truly receives Christ as his Savior, God wants him to know, that he's saved. How can a person know that he's saved? He can know by:

1-Believing God's Word.
2-By the witness of the Holy Spirit.

A good verse to use for assurance is found, in (John 3:36) it says, "He that believeth on the Son hath everlasting life, and he that believeth not the

Son shall not see life, but the wrath of God abideth on him."

Note that God speaks of two groups, of people in this verse, those who believe in the Son, and those who don't believe in Him. What does God say, about those who believe in the Son? He that believeth in the Son, "*hath*" everlasting life. The word *hath* means, that you have it right, now!

Now, turn to (l John 5:11-13) it says, "And this is the record, that God hath given to us eternal life, and this life is in His Son." In (Verse 12) it says, "He that hath the Son hath life, and he that hath not the Son of God hath not life." In (Verse 13) it says, "These things have I written unto you that believe on the name of the Son of God, that ye may know that ye have eternal life, and that ye may believe on the name of the Son of God." Notice in these verses that God says, that we can *know,* that we have eternal life. God said it! I believe it! And that settles it!

Assurance of Salvation also comes from the witness of the Holy Spirit. This, simply means that the Holy Spirit, let's us know in our spirit, that we are saved.

The Bible says, in (Romans 8:16) "The Spirit itself beareth witness with our spirit, that we are the children of God."

How can we know that another person is saved? We can't know for sure. We may sincerely believe that a person has received Christ as their Savior, but we may be, mistaken. For this reason, we should *never,* tell a person, that he is saved. This is the work of the Holy Spirit.

Your Way is Not God's Way

In seeking to win a person to Christ, you must be bold, yet you must be tactful and courteous. You, must turn the conversation to spiritual matters without causing offense.

Next, you must find out what a person believes, about the way of Salvation. One way to do this is to ask questions. If, someone were to ask you, how can I become a child of God? What would you say? Most unsaved people think that a person becomes a Christian, by being baptized, joining a Church, or by doing good deeds. These things are good, but they don't save anyone. The Bible says, in (Ephesians 2:8-9) "For by grace are ye saved through faith, and that not of yourselves, it is the gift of God." In (Verse 9) it says, "Not of works, lest any man should boast." After, you have explained this, you can ask, "would you like for me to show you from the Bible, what God says about how a person is saved?" If the answer is "*yes*" then you can proceed with the four steps in leading a person to Christ.

The essential quality of a soul winner, is love for people. You can't win souls, if you don't love souls. God, loves all people, for all are precious in His sight. Ask God to fill your heart with His love. Now, can children be saved? Yes, they surely can! In fact, it is much easier for children, to trust the Lord Jesus as their Savior, than it is for grown-ups. The Lord Jesus told us, in (Matthew 18:3) "And said, Verily I say unto you, except ye be converted, and become as little children, ye shall not enter into the Kingdom of Heaven." In (Matthew 18:5-6,) it says, "And whoso shall receive one such little child in my name receiveth me." In (Verse 6) "But whoso shall offend one of these little ones which believe in me, it were better for him that a millstone were hanged about his neck, and that he was drowned in the depth of the sea." *So don't neglect the children.* How old does a child have to be to be saved? Old enough to know, right from wrong. How do we lead a child to Christ? Simply show him/her from God's Word, that he/she has sinned and that he/she needs a Savior. Then tell him/her about the Savior who died for his/her sins and ask him/her to receive Jesus unto him/her heart.

Now, let me say this, "you will have people, who will have objections." I'm going to list twelve objections, that will help you in this area.

First, use your Bible to answer there objections:

1-I'm not a great sinner! God says, "that we are all sinners." In (Romans 3:23) it says, "For all have sinned, and come short of the Glory of God."

2-I'm a Baptist, a Methodist, and a Catholic etc. Church membership, doesn't save anyone, you must be born again. Jesus said, in (John 3:3) "Jesus answered and said unto him, verily,verily, I say unto thee, Except a man be born again, he can not see the Kingdom of God."

3-There are hypocrites in the Church! Yes, there are, but there'll be No hypocrites in Heaven. You'll not be judged by what someone else did, but by your own life. In (Romans 14:12) it says, "So then everyone of us shall give account of *himself* to God."

4-I would have to give up too much! If you're not willing to give up your sins, you will be lost forever. Is it worth this? Jesus said, in (Mark 8:36) "For what shall it profit a man, if he shall gain the whole world, and lose his own soul?"

5-I'm waiting until I become better! You can't make yourself better. The Lord Jesus, tells us to come to Him, just as we are and He promises to receive us. He said, in (John 6:37) "All that the Father giveth me shall come to me, and him that cometh to me I will in no wise cast out."

6-I'm afraid I can't live a Christian life! No one can, until Christ comes to live in your heart. He, enables us to live the Christian life. The Apostle Paul said, in (Philippians 4:13) "I can do all things through Christ which strengtheneth me."

7-I'm too great of a sinner! He will save anyone who comes to Him. The Apostle Paul said, in (l Timothy 1:15) "This is a faithful saying, and worthy of all acceptation, that Christ Jesus came into the world to save sinners, of whom I am chief."

8-I'm doing the best I can! We're not saved by our good works, but through faith in Christ. In (Ephesians 2:8-9) it says, "For by grace are ye saved through faith, and that not of yourselves, it is the gift of God." In (Verse 9) it says, "Not of works, lest any man should boast."

9-I think one way is as good as another, as long as you are sincere! You may be sincere, but you may be sincerely, wrong. The Bible says, in (Proverbs 14:12) "There is a way which seemeth right into a man, but the end thereof are the ways of death." Jesus is our Savior. We can't come to God except by Him. Jesus said, in (John 14:6) "Jesus saith unto him, I am the way, the truth, and the life, no man cometh unto the Father, but by me."

10-Maybe later! It's dangerous to put off such, an important decision. The Bible says, in (Proverbs 27:1) "Boast not thyself of tomorrow, for thou knowest not what a day bring forth."

11-I don't want to give up my sins! Then, "*You, will be lost forever.*" Jesus said, in (Luke 13:5) "I tell you, nay, but, except ye repent, ye shall all likewise perish."

12-I don't believe in Hell! This, doesn't change the fact of, *hell.* The Bible says, in (Revelation 21:8) "But the fearful, and unbelieving, and the abominable, and murderers, and whoremongers, and sorcerers, and idolaters, and all liars, shall have their part in the lake which burneth with fire and brimstone: which is a second death."

Memorize these objections and the answers, so you will know them, when you need them. Now, I have some "do's and don'ts" which are very important, also. *Do*-Always use your Bible, when leading people to Christ. Even, though you may be able to quote the verse, it's better to let the other person read it himself. *Don't*-Use too many verses. *Do*-Look to God in prayer for the guidance of the Holy Spirit. *Don't*-Interrupt people. Try to find out their problems, but don't get side tracked. Keep bringing them back to the matter of their relationship to the Lord Jesus. *Do*-Be earnest. This is no time for joking. Soul winning is serious business. *Don't*-Argue. God doesn't send us out to win arguments, he sends us out to win souls. *Do*-Be careful of your breath. Don't offend people, by having bad breath. *Do*-Admit it, when you don't know the answer to a question. Just say, I don't know the answer to that question, but I'm sure there must be one. One thing I do know, Jesus Christ changed my life, and He will do the same for you. Do-Value every person highly. We must see every person as one for whom Christ died. If we look down or despise anyone, we aren't worthy to be Christ's servants. *Don't*-Be discouraged. Some, will reject the Savior, but keep right on witnessing for Christ. *Do*-Be concerned. Jesus wept and prayed over lost souls and so should we. *Do*-Encourage new converts, to confess Christ to others and to join a Bible believing Church at the first opportunity.

Now, this is one area in life that affects a lot of people, and that's overcoming your fears. One of the greatest hindrances to personal works is the fear of people. We're afraid of what others will think.

A Christian, who was a fearless personal worker, was asked, "if he had always been bold?" His reply, was "he had once been as timid, as anyone else." Then, one day he couldn't stand it any longer. He fell on his knees, with his Bible opened, to (Psalms 34:4) it says, "I sought the Lord, and He heard me, and delivered me from all my fears." As he prayed, he said, "Lord you did this for David. Do it now for me." God heard his prayer and answered it. Ask God, to do the same for you.

You have the message that brings eternal life to people, and you must tell it, without any fear.

When, we are fearful of people, we make them out, to be bigger than, the Gospel message itself. You can win souls for Christ. There're people all around you, who need to be saved.

1-Begin, now to pray for them.
2-Watch for an opportunity to witness to them.
3-Learn the four basic truths of the Gospel.
4-Learn how to answer objections.
5-Be ready and God will use you. Don't be afraid of making mistakes.

You will make the greatest mistake of all, if you don't try to win someone to Christ. Remember this, through Christ *all things* are possible. In (ll Corinthians 12:9) it says, "And he said unto me, My grace is sufficient for thee: for my strength is made perfect in weakness. Most gladly therefore will I rather glory in my infirmities, that the power of Christ may rest upon me."

Your Way is Not God's Way

The saddest experience in the life of a Christian, is to be under the power of sin. Sin, in the life of a Christian has three terrible results.

1- It dishonors the name of the, Lord Jesus. If you're a Christian, you represent the Lord Jesus. When you yield to sin, you bring dishonor to His name.
2- It robs you of your joy and power. As, long as you are yielding to sin, God will not use you.
3- It destroys your Christian testimony. Other people judge your Christian witness, not so much by what you say, but by the way you live, day by day.

Chapter 17

Right now, by your life, you are saying, one of two things to other people. You're saying, the Christian life works, or you're saying the Christian life doesn't work. The way you live as a Christian, affects not only your life, but the lives of other people as well.

Do you see why it's so important, for you to be a victorious Christians? What's the victorious life? When we speak of "the victorious life" we're not speaking of a life without temptation or a life of sinless perfection. It's not possible for a person to have such a transaction with the Lord, as to enable him to say, I'm without sin, or I can never sin, again. The Bible says, in (l John 1:8) "If we saythat we have *no sin*, we deceive ourselves, and the truth is not in us." What then, *is the victorious life*? It's, a life of, peace and joy in the Lord. It's a life of, constant fellowship with the Lord. It's a life of, victory over sins, even the so called "little sins" such as temper, fault finding, irritability, complaining, lack of love, envy, jealousy, unkind words, wrong thoughts, worry, and anxiety are just to name a few.

The victorious life, is a life that Glorifies Him. Then, who can have this kind of life? Any believer? It's for you! The victorious life isn't for just a few, special Christians. It's presented in the New Testament, as the normal Christian life. God has made provision for every Christian to live, this kind of life.

Let's see what the Bible says, about it. The life of victory, is that it's a gift. Just as eternal life is a gift, so is the victorious life. It can't be earned, and it's the gift from God. The Bible says, in (I Corinthians 15:57) "But thanks be to God, which giveth us the victory through our Lord Jesus Christ." Victory, is by God's grace.

What is grace? Grace, is something God does for us. Grace has often been defined as, "God's unmerited favor" but grace is much more than this. Grace is God's mighty, omnipotent power working for us, doing for us, what we could never do for, ourselves. >From beginning to end, our Salvation is *All* of Gods grace.

But, do we have a part in Salvation? Yes, we do. What is our part? Our part is to *receive* what Gods grace provides for us. Now, let's consider our Salvation, and see the part God's Grace, has in it. First, let's think about the time God saved us. Each one of us, can look back to a time, when we were separated from God and dead in trespasses and sins. But, God loved us and saved us by His grace. The Bible says, in (Ephesians 2:1) "And you hath he

Your Way is Not God's Way

quickened, who were dead in trespasses and sins." When we're "lead in trespasses and sin" could we make ourselves alive spiritually? *No*, we couldn't. It was God's power working in us, that made us alive, spiritually. It was *all of* God's Grace. The Bible says, in (Ephesians 2:8) "For by grace are ye saved through faith, and that not of yourselves, it is the gift of God."

Now, let's think about the future. We know that, one day, the Lord Jesus is coming for His believers. *All* believers, both those who have died and those who are living when He comes, we will be caught up to meet the Lord in the air. What a wonderful day that will be. Our *bodies* will be changed, instantly, and we shall be made like Him. The Bible says, in (I Thessalonians 4:16-18) "For the Lord Himself shall descend from Heaven with a shout, with the voice of the archangel, and with the trump of God, and the dead in Christ shall rise first." Which means our dead, loved ones will rise first, Oh Glory, in (Verse 17) it says, "Then we which are alive and remain shall be caught up together with them in the clouds, to meet the Lord in the air, and so shall we ever be with the Lord." In (Verse 18) it says, "Wherefore comfort one another with these words." *My! My! My!* What a reunion that's going to be, you and I, our loved ones, and the Lord Jesus. "If I don't know anything, else, I do know that!" I can't wait for our Lord Jesus, to come back to get His beloved children. Oh! Thank you, Jesus, for your wonderful blessings, that are yet to come.

Your Way is Not God's Way

It reminds me of the old song, we use to sing in Church, when I was just a small boy, "Oh, how I love Jesus, Oh, how I love Jesus...because He first loved me." Thank you, Lord.

Will we be caught up to meet the Lord, by our own power? No, not at all. It'll be by God's, almighty power. What about now? Are we just to struggle along in our own strength, doing the best we can, but failing miserably? No! God has made it possible, for us to be victorious, *now*. What's God's provision for us, now? His provision is, *His grace*, His mighty power working in us. No matter, what our situation may be. God says, to us "My grace is sufficient for you."

I just can't help myself, as I'm writing this, I sit here just full of joy, weeping, my heart is full of gladness, and thankfulness, at the plans He has for all of His believers. He loves us so much, one day we all, will sit at His supper table, to eat with Him. Thank you, Heavenly Father for all our blessings.

Like I said, before "**Your Way is Not God's Way**!" God's grace for us now, is simply, Christ living in us. When God says, "my grace is sufficient for you," He's saying, "my Christ is sufficient for you." Trust Him. He can give you victory in every situation, no matter what it is. What do we do? We rest in Christ. We trust and obey Him, to keep us and to give us victory. This is receiving God's Grace. When we do this, we reign in life. The Bible says, in (Romans 5:17) "For if by one man's offence death reigned by one, much more they which receive abundance of grace and of the gift of righteousness shall reign in life by one, Jesus Christ." By His grace, we reign in this life, by His grace. Victory is in Jesus Christ.

For many Christians, are seeking victory through teaching or some unusual experience, but victory isn't in a teaching or in an experience. No, victory is in the, Lord Jesus Christ. The Bible says, in (I Corinthians 15:57) "But thanks be to God, which giveth us the victory through our Lord Jesus Christ."

Jesus Christ makes two offers to every, person:

1-He, offers them eternal life.
2-He, offers them victory over sin.

He makes both of these offers on exactly the same basis, that we let, Him do it all. Both are gifts- Both are in Christ.

Just, as there's a right way and a wrong way to seek Salvation so, there's a right way and a wrong way to seek victory. The wrong way, is to try to do it yourself. The right way is to let the Lord do it for you. And the Lord knows, I need *all* the help I can get, so I'll just, let the Lord do it for, me. The Lord Jesus said, in (Matthew 11:28) "Come unto me, all ye that labor and are heavy laden, and *I will give you rest.*" If you were working at a job, and the Lord Jesus came to you and said "I will give you rest,"what would you expect Him to do? You, would expect Him to take over your job, and do it while you rested. This is exactly what He wants to do for you. Perhaps you have been trying to live the victorious life, but failing. The Lord Jesus, says to you "Let me take over." I will live the victorious life in and through you. How do we enter the life of victory? The conditions for entering the life of victory are just two:

1-Commit yourself to Christ.
2-Take Christ as your victory.

Now, let's consider these two conditions:

1-You must commit yourself, all you are, and all you have, to the Lord Jesus. If you keep control of your life, then you'e responsible for keeping yourself. If you commit yourself to the Lord Jesus, then it becomes, *His responsibility* to keep. The Apostle Paul said, in (II Timothy 1:12) "For the which cause I also suffer these things, nevertheless I am not ashamed, for I know whom I have believed, and am persuaded that He's able to keep that which I have committed unto Him against that day." The Lord Jesus, was able to keep Paul and to give Him victory, but the Apostle Paul had done something that enabled the Lord to do this. What was it? Paul, committed himself completely to the Lord Jesus. If you want the Lord, to keep you and to give you victory, you must commit yourself to Him.

Is there anything in your life at this time, that you have been holding back from the Lord? If so, will you give it to Him right, now? Turn over the past to Him, with all it's sins and failures. Commit the future, to

Him with *all* of it's unknowns. Commit your dear loved ones to Him, that young man or woman you love. Tell God that, if they aren't part of His plans for you, you're willing for them, to pass out of your life. Tell Him right now, that you turn yourself over to Him, all that you are, and all that you have, for now and for eternity. When you do this, you will have taken the first step toward victory. Will you do it right now? You, will never have a victorious life, until Jesus Christ, has *all* there is of you.

2-You must take Christ as your victory. Taking Christ, as your victory is alot like taking Him, as your Savior. What did you do, when you took Christ as your savior? You came to Him, as a helpless sinner, and you trusted Him to, save you. Now, what do you do, when you take Christ as your victory? You, come to Him as a helpless, defeated Christian, and you trust Him to give you victory. Will you take Him as your victory right, now? Let's pray, just say to Him, *"Lord Jesus, I have tried and tried, to live the Christian life, but I have failed. Right now, I take you as my victory. I trust you to give us victory. And, I accept it in your Holy name." Amen.*

When, you took Christ as your Savior, how did you know, that God had saved you? *By His Word*! You, took God at His Word, and you thanked Him, for saving you. When you take Christ as your victory, how do you know that God has given you victory?

By *His Word*! What does God say? He says, "*My Grace, My Christ*, is sufficient for you." Will you take God, at His Word and thank Him, on the basis of His Word, that His Grace *is* sufficient for you? Thank Him, that Christ is actually living in your heart, and that, at this very moment, He's meeting *all* your needs. When you surrender to Christ and take Him as your victory, you have entered the life of victory. You can say, I know my Lord Jesus is meeting all my needs, right now, because His Grace *is* sufficient for me. How do you continue in victory? You enter into victory, by yielding, to Christ and trusting Him as your victory. You continue in victory, by continuing to yield to Christ and continuing to trust Him as your victory. Victory isn't a once, in a life time, matter. It's taking Christ as your victory, moment-by-moment. Your attitude becomes, one of depending, on Him, moment-by-moment. Remember, victory is by God's Grace. It's not gritting your teeth and struggling to keep yourself under control. It's a miracle of God's grace. It's not *trying*, but *trusting*. Trying, is what we do, trusting, is letting the Lord, do it for us. Will you ever fail again? Yes, there'll be failures as you learn to walk in victory. As I have already said, "the victorious life isn't a life without sin." What will happen when we fail? Will you be discouraged and think, "I can't be a victorious Christian. It's alright, for others but, not for me?" Now, this is just what the Devil wants you to think. *Don't think it!*

Have you ever seen a baby learning to walk? What happens? He/she takes a few steps, and he/she falls down. Then what? Does, he/she just lie, on the floor and say, "it's no use. I just can't walk. I'll never learn to walk?" No, he doesn't, do this. What does he do? He has a good cry, then he/she gets up and tries to walk, again. He/she has other tumbles, but he/she keeps at it, until he/she learns to walk.

This is the way it is, in the Christian life. While you are learning to walk in victory, you will have many falls. What should you do when you fall? *Get up*! Confess, your sins to the Lord. Tell Him, that you didn't mean to fall. Tell Him, that you want to live a life of victory. Then, start again. Walk once more, trusting Christ as your victory. As, time goes on, you will find you aren't falling so, often. Don't accept defeat. When you fall, you should never remain in defeat. You, can be instantly restored to your place of victory. How? By confessing your sins to God and, once again, claiming Christ as your victor. Remember, Christ hasn't failed. He's still the victorious one, and He lives in you. You can have victory. Anything, that Jesus Christ has ever done for any of His Disciples, He'll do for you. God, means for you to live victoriously. You must believe that the life of victory is meant for you, right here, and right now, in your circumstances.

    1-Choose the life of victory. The life of a defeated Christian is hard. The only life that honors the Lord Jesus, is a victorious life.

    2-Take the steps of victory. Commit yourself to Christ. Take Him as your victory.

    3-Trust Christ moment-by-moment. In every situation, depend on Him, say "I know my

Your Way is Not God's Way

Lord Jesus is meeting all my needs, right now, because His Grace is sufficient for me."

Chapter 18

❦

In (Matthew 24:42) it says, "Watch therefore, for ye know not what hour your Lord doth come." Jesus is coming again! How do we know? Because He said, so in, (John 14:2-3) "In my Father's house are many mansions, if it were not so, I would of told you. I go to prepare a place for you." In (Verse 3) it says, "And if I go and prepare a place for you, I will come again, and receive you unto myself, that where I am, there ye may be also."

When, the Bible speaks, of the coming of the Lord, it's not speaking of death. Oh No! Nor, is it speaking of the coming of the Holy Spirit. It's speaking, of the *"Personal-Visible"* coming of the Lord Jesus Christ. At the time of Christ's ascension, while the Disciples stood watching Him go up into Heaven, two angels appeared to them. In (Acts 1:11) it says, "Which also said, Ye men of Galilae, who stand ye gazing up into Heaven? This same Jesus, which is taken up from you into Heaven, shall so come in like manner as ye have seen Him go into Heaven." How will Jesus come? He'll will come in the same manner in which

He ascended into Heaven. The Disciples saw Jesus go back into Heaven, and those who are living, when He comes again, will see Him, then.

When is Jesus coming? What will happen when He comes? What will happen to the unbelievers and to the Christians, when the Lord comes, again? These are very important questions, and in the following pages, I will explain these important questions, as the Lord leads me. Does, any man know the exact time of the Lord's coming? No! The Lord Jesus said, "But of that day and hour knoweth no man." Since, we don't know exactly when the Lord is coming, we should be ready for His coming at *all times*.

The proper attitude of a Christian, is to always be looking for the coming of the, Lord Jesus. What are the signs of Jesus coming? Though, we can't know the exact time when Jesus will come, we do know, that He is coming very soon. How do we know this? By the signs, which the Bible gives concerning the time of his coming.

Now, let us see how, these signs are being fulfilled. In (Matthew 24:6-7) it says, "And ye shall hear of wars and rumors of wars, see that ye be not troubled, for all these things must come to pass, but the end is not yet." In (Verse 7) it says, "For nations shall rise against nations, and kingdom against kingdom, and there shall be famines, and pestilences and earthquakes, in divers places."

> 1-Wars: There have already been wars, but Jesus said, "that the end times would be marked by a great increase in the number of wars." He

said, "For nation shall rise against nation, and kingdom against kingdom." Since World War II, there have been more than 45 wars, 12 of them major in scope.

2-Famines: The Lord Jesus said, "There shall be famines, and pestilences and earthquakes in divers places." Never, before in history has scientists recorded so many earthquakes, as they have in the last 25 years.

3-Israel: 600 years before the time of Christ, Israel ceased to exist as a nation. The Jews, were scattered to the ends of the earth. But, the Bible prophesized that God, would bring His people back into their, land in the last days, and that the desert which had lain barren for so long would "blossom like a rose." This has been fulfilled.

4-Jerusalem: The Lord Jesus, gave an even more specific sign of the end time. This sign concerns the city of Jerusalem. The Lord Jesus said, in (Luke 21:24) "And they shall fall by the edge of the sword, and shall be led away captive into all nations, and Jerusalem shall be trodden down of the Gentiles, until the times of the Gentiles be fulfilled." Jerusalem has been controlled by the Gentiles, those who weren't Jews, for about 1,900 years. But, in 1967 the Israelites captured the city of Jerusalem. Jerusalem, is now controlled by the Jews. This is another sign that the coming of the Lord Jesus is near.

5-Ten Kingdoms: The Bible says that, "in the last days, there will be a confederation of ten nations out of what was the old Roman Empire." The European common market appears to be this confederation. In (Daniel 2:44) it says, "And in the days of these kings shall the God of Heaven set up a kingdom, which shall never be destroyed, and the kingdom shall not be left to other people, but it shall break in pieces and consume all these kingdoms, and it shall stand forever."

6-Peace efforts: Another sign of the last days, is the great increase in peace conferences. But, peace efforts have failed and will continue to fail until Jesus comes. He's the prince of peace, and there'll will be no peace, in the world until He is reigning. The Bible says, in (Isaiah 33:7) "Behold, their valiant ones shall cry without, the ambassadors of peace shall weep bitterly."

7-Travel and knowledge: The Bible says, that at the time of the end, in (Daniel 12:4) it says, "But thou, O Daniel, shut up the words, and seal the book, even to the time of the end, many shall run to and fro, and knowledge shall be increased."

8-Great wickedness: The world isn't getting better, instead, it's getting much worse. This is a fulfillment of the words of the Lord Jesus, in (Luke 17:26) it says, "And as it was in the days of Noah so shall it be also in the days of the son of man." What was it like in the days of Noah? It was a time of great wickedness on the earth. Let's look in, (Genesis 6:5) the Bible says, "And God saw that the wickedness of man was great in the earth, and that every imagination of the thoughts of his heart was only evil continually."

9-Spiritism, witchcraft: The current interest in horoscopes, fortune tellers, witchcraft, and spiritism is another sign that we are living in the last days. The Bible says, in (I Timothy 4:1) "Now the Spirit speaketh expressly, that in the latter times some shall depart from the faith, giving heed to seducing spirits, and doctrines of Devils."

10-Apostasy: The Bible, tells us that the last days, just before Jesus comes, will be marked by great apostasy. The word "apostasy" means, *a falling away from the truth*. This prophecy has been fulfilled in many of the seminaries and Bible Schools, the teachers and professors, no longer believe that the Bible, is the inspired, Word of God. Sad, but true, these men make light of the miracles, deny the virgin birth of Christ, deny that Jesus Christ is God, and destroy the faith of those they teach. This is a warning. Don't stay under the teaching of those who deny the great truths, of the Bible. The Bible says, in (Proverbs 19:27) "Cease, my Son, to hear the instruction that causeth to err from the words of knowledge." There's great apostasy in many Churches, also. Many ministers who claim to be servants of Christ, no longer preach the Gospel. They no longer preach that we are lost sinners and need to be saved, through faith, in the blood of Christ. Instead, these men deny the necessity of the new birth, (being saved) and preach that God is the Father of all men, and that all men are brothers. The Bible says, "From such turn away." Also, in (l Timothy 4:1) it says, "Now the spirit speaketh expressly, that in the latter times some shall depart from the faith, giving heed to seducing, spirits, and doctrines of Devils." I know this seems very harsh, but it's so true, and I have to write the truth, as the Lord lays it on my heart. So, be very careful in this area, for the Devil is working overtime, to steal souls away from God.

So what do these signs tell us? They, tell us that "*Jesus is coming soon*!" He could come this very day, or anytime, soon. The Lord Jesus said, in (Luke 21:31) "So likewise ye, when ye see these things come to pass, know ye that the Kingdom of God is nigh at hand." What will happen when Jesus comes? First, the Lord Jesus will. come *secretly,* to take His Church out of the world. In a moment, "in the twinkling of an eye." Now that's very quick, every believer will be caught up, to meet our Lord. Just makes me want to jump up and down with joy!

So, what will the world be like when all the Christians are gone? It will be a world without decency and restraint. Evil and wickedness will abound as never before. At this time, an extraordinary man will appear on the earth. He'll possess great leadership ability and marvelous powers. He'll even be able to call down fire down from Heaven. But, his power won't come from God, his power will come from *Satan*. The Bible calls this man "*The Antichrist*." The word "anti" means against. For he is against God and against, Christ through deceit and His miraculous powers. Satan's antichrist will gain control of the whole world. *No one,,* will be able to buy or sell without his mark. He will set up a great image and require people to worship him and his image. Those who refuse to do so, will be killed. The antichrist will rule the world. The first part of the antichrist's reign, will be a time of great prosperity on the earth. This will last about three and a half years. Then, will come a time of great trouble and distress as God will pour out His wrath on the wicked, Christ's rejecting world. This terrible time is called "the great tribulation." The Bible say's that, at this time, there will be disturbances in the Heavens. The sun will turn black, the moon will turn blood red. On, earth will be plagues, diseases, earthquakes, and famines. One third of the inhabitants of the world will be killed. One, might think that those, who had heard and Rejected the Gospel, before, would surely repent of their sins and turn to Christ, during the great tribulation, but they won't. The Bible says, in (ll Thessalonians 2:10-12) "And with all deceivableness of unrighteousness in them that perish, because they received not the *love of the truth*, that they might be saved." In (Verse 11) it says, "And for this cause God shall send them strong delusion, that they should believeth a lie." In (Verse 12) it says,"That they all might be damned who believeth not the truth, but had pleasure in unrighteousness." Also, in (Revelations 9:20-21) it says, "And the rest of the men which were not killed by these plagues yet repented not of the works of their hands, that they should not worship Devils, and idols of gold, and silver, and brass, and stone, and of wood, which neither can see, nor hear, nor walk." In (Verse 21) it says, "Neither repented they of their murders, nor of their sorceries, nor of their fornication, nor of their thefts." It's indeed a serious thing to, *Rejected the Gospel.* Following the terrible events of the great tribulation, the Lord Jesus will return to earth in great power and glory. He will destroy His enemies, and set up His Kingdom here on earth. The Bible says, in (ll Thessalonians 1:7-8) "And to you who are troubled rest with us, when the Lord Jesus shall be revealed from Heaven with His mighty angels." In (Verse 8) it says, "In flaming fire taking vengeance on them that *know not God,* and that obey not the Gospel of our Lord Jesus Christ." We know without a doubt, that the Lord Jesus is coming back again, *real soon!* For the unbelievers, the coming of the Lord Jesus will be a time of terror and judgment.

But, for the Christians, the coming of the Lord is associated with the word "hope."

1-It's, a blessed hope when Jesus comes, He'll change our bodies, to be like His glorious resurrected body. This will take place in an instant. Then, we shall be forever with our *Lord.* The

Bible says, in (Titus 2:13) "Looking for that blessed *hope*, and the glorious appearing of the great God and our savior Jesus Christ." Let's also, look at (Verses 14-15) "Who gave Himself for us, that He might redeem us from all iniquity, and purify unto Himself a peculiar people, zealous of good works." In (Verse 15) it says, "These things speak, and exhort, and rebuke with *all* authority. Let no man despise thee."

2- It's, a comforting hope. The unbelieving people bury their loved ones, with no hope of ever seeing them again. But, not so with the Christians. When Jesus comes. Our loved ones who died trusting Him, will be raised from the dead, and we shall be *reunited,* with them, forever. What a comforting hope we have in the Lord Jesus.

3- It's a purifying hope. The Christian who truly believes that the coming of the Lord is near "purifies himself," meaning that, he's getting himself ready for the Lord's, coming. Why? Because he knows, that he'll soon stand before the Lord Jesus, to give an account of his life. The Bible says, in (ll Corinthians 5:10) "For we must *all* appear before the judgment seat of Christ, that everyone may receive the things done in his body, according to that he hath done, whether it be good or bad." At the judgment seat of Christ, we'll be judged for what we have done *after* we were saved. You know, this will be a solemn occasion for all believers. What are some of the things the Lord will judge us by in that day? He'll judge us by, how much of His Word, we have learned and obeyed. He'll judge us, by our obedience or lack of obedience to the great commission. He'll call us before Him and say, "I committed the Gospel to you, what did you do that others, might be saved?" He'll judge us by how, we have used our time, our abilities, and our money. Some believers, will be found to be faithful servants, and will receive great rewards, from the Lord. Others, will be found to be unfaithful servants and will be dealt with as, such. Perhaps some of us will wish that we could live our lives over again, but the truth is, we only have one life.

What we do for the Lord, we must do right, now. Will you be ready? What can I do for my Savior before He comes? How can I glorify Him? How should my time, money and my abilities be used for Him? These are some very important questions, that should concern every serious-minded, Christians.

If you truly believe that Jesus is coming soon, here are some things, that the Lord has put on my heart, that we all should do:

1-Do the job at hand. God has a job for you right, now. Do it well. When God has something different for you to do, He will show it to you.
2-Grow in grace and knowledge of the Lord Jesus. You, do this by prayer and Bible study and by serving the Lord.

3-Prepare yourself to serve God. Learn God's Word. Memorize scriptures. Keep your daily quiet time. (Prayer time)
4-Win others to the Lord Jesus.
5-Deny yourself and live for the Lord Jesus, and for others. This is the secret of a *fruitful life*.
6-Maintain Christian fellowship with other believers. You should belong to and faithfully support a local, Bible believing Church. There're many other prophecies in the Bible, concerning, Christ. Some of them have to do with His, second coming. These haven't been fulfilled as yet, but they'll be fulfilled when Jesus comes again. What do these scriptures tell us? They tell us that Jesus is the Christ, the promised Savior.

In the Gospel of John he makes it clear, that Jesus is the Christ. In (John 20:30-31) it says, "And many other signs truly did Jesus in the presence of His Disciples, which are not written is this Book." In (Verse 31) it says, "But these are written, that ye might believe that Jesus is the Christ, the Son of God, and that believing ye might have life through His name." We must believe on the Lord Jesus Christ. Over and over the Lord Jesus, emphasized one thing, that men must believe in Him, in order to be saved. Jesus said, to the Jews, of His day, in (John 8:24) "I said therefore unto you, that ye shall die in your sins, for if ye believe not that I am He, ye shall die in your sins."

I've talked a lot about the "Lord Jesus Christ." Now I'm going to explain the meaning of each:

Lord- this is His kingly name that stands for His rulership over all things. He is God. He has all power in Heaven and in the earth.

Jesus- this is His personal, human name. it means, "Savior" Jesus is the Savior, the one who died for our sins and rose again from the dead. He *is* a living Savior.

Christ- this is His official name, it means "the anointed one." We have already seen that Jesus is *"The Christ"* the promised Savior.

Chapter 19

What does it mean to believe in the Lord Jesus Christ?

1-That He *is* the Son of God.
2-That He died on the cross for our sins and rose, again.
3-That by believing in Him, He becomes your very own Savior, so that, what He has done is really for you.

Remember, believing God, means believing precisely what God says, in His Word. Jesus is the Christ, the promised Savior. If you have Him, you have eternal life. In (John 3:16) it says, "For God so loved the world, that He gave His only begotten Son, that whosoever believes in Him should not perish, but have everlasting life." In (I John 5:11-12) it says, "And this is the record, that God has given to us eternal life, and this life is in His Son." In (Verse 12) it says, "He that hath the Son hath life, and He that hath not the Son of God hath not life." In (John

1:12) it says, "But as many as received Him to them gave he power to become the Sons of God, even to them that believe His name." In (Romans 5:8) it reads, "But God commendeth His love toward us, in that, while we were yet sinners, Christ died for us." In (I John 4:14) it says, "And we have seen and do testify that the Father sent the Son to be the Saviour of the world." So yes, Jesus is God. In (John 5:22-23) it says, "For the Father judgeth no man, but hath committed all judgment unto the Son." In (Verse 23) it says, "That all men should honor the Son, even as they honor the Father. He that honoureth not the Son honoureth not the Father which has sent Him." He has always been God. He *will* always be God.

But, He did come as a man. The Lord Jesus, is sometimes called "the God-Man." This is a very good name for Him, because He *is* truly God, and *was* truly a, man. Because, He lived on this earth as a man, the Lord Jesus understands us perfectly. He knows, what it's like to be tempted, to be misunderstood, and to be hated, to be poor, to be hungry, and to suffer persecution. Because He was a man, He knows what it's like when, we suffer and are tempted.

For He *is* God. He's wonderfully able to help us when we call on Him, because of who Jesus is and what He has done, there is *Great power* in His name. Jesus is powerful in:

1-The Salvation of men.
2-In our prayers.
3-In the warfare against Satan.

The Bible says, in (Romans 10:13) "For whosoever shall call upon the name of the Lord shall be saved." If you aren't saved, take the Lord at His word and call upon His name. Open your heart's to Him and say, "O Lord Jesus! Confess your sins to Him. Thank Him, for loving you and for dying for your sins. Ask, Him to come into your heart and be your Savior. He'll hear you and save you." In (John 6:37) it says, "All that the Father giveth me shall come to me, and Him that cometh to me I will in no wise cast out." We should always pray to the Father, in *Jesus name*. His, name has great power.

The Bible, tells us about a lame man, who lay at the gate of the temple begging. Each day, someone had to carry him to the temple. When the Apostle Peter, saw him, he said, "silver and gold, have I none, but such as I have I give thee, in the name of Jesus Christ of Nazareth, rise up and walk." The man leaped up, and walked and went into the temple with them, praising God. When, people wondered how the man had been healed, Peter told them that it was by the power of Jesus. Peter said, in (Acts 3:16) "And His name through faith in His name hath made this man strong, whom ye see and know: yea, the faith which is by Him hath given Him this perfect soundness in the presence of you all."

Just how, wonderful is the name of Jesus? Begin now to pray to the Father in Jesus name. Pray for your unsaved friends and loved ones. Pray about everything that concerns you. The Lord Jesus said, in (John 16:24) "Hitherto have ye asked nothing in my name: ask, and ye shall receive, that your joy may be full." Begin now to call upon the name of the Lord Jesus. Whatever your needs are, you can call upon Him. He's the mighty Son of God and He loves you. He wants you to call upon Him. The Lord says, in (Psalms 50:15) "And call upon me in the day of trouble, I will deliver thee, and thou shalt glorify me." Jesus is a mighty God! We can call on Him and He will help us. There's no better help in the world, than the help from the Lord Jesus, Christ. I have always wondered, what Heaven would be like, and I am sure you have, also? The Lord is coming to take His believers to be with Him. For those of us who have trusted Christ as Savior, His coming will be a glorious time. He's coming to take us to be with Him, forever! And you know, it's a promise, that will never be *broken*. Oh! Thank you, Lord. First, we'll go to Heaven with the Lord to be judged, for what we have done, after we were saved. Those, who have faithfully served the Lord will receive wonderful *rewards*. The Bible, is full of these blessed wonderful rewards. Later, we'll return to this earth with the, Lord Jesus. When He comes in great power and glory to destroy His enemies, and to set up *His kingdom*. We'll reign with Him for 1,000 years. Then, we'll go to be with the Lord, in Heaven, for ever and ever. It, reminds me of another song, we all sang in Church, "Oh! Victory in Jesus, my Savior forever, He bought me and He sought me, through His redeming blood...." Oh Glory! Thank you Jesus!

Chapter 20

❦

Now, let's consider three things about Heaven:

1-Heaven is a city of beauty. Heaven is more beautiful than we can ever imagine. The Apostle John said, in (Revelation 21:2) "And I John saw the Holy City, New Jerusalem, coming down from God out of Heaven, prepared as a bride adorned for her husband." The world, has never seen a city, like this one, for the builder and maker, of this city is God, Himself. John, describes it as having, *"The Glory of God."* John, wrote in (Revelation 21:11, 12,18) it says, "Having the glory of God, and her light was like unto a stone most precious, even like a jasper stone, clear as crystal." In (Verse 12) it says, "And had a wall great and high, and had twelve gates, and at the gates twelve angles, and names written thereon, which are the names of the twelve tribes of the children of Israel." In (Verse 18) it says, "And the building of the wall of it was of jasper, and the city was pure gold, like unto clear glass." Just think, this city is made of pure gold, clear as glass. The foundations of the city are covered, with all manner of precious stones. There are twelve gates, and each gate is a huge, beautiful pearl. Even, the streets of the city is made of pure gold. The builder (and maker) of this city is *"God Himself."* This city, has no need for the sun or the moon. God the Father, and God the Son, will fill this city with light. The Bible says, in (Revelation 21:23-24) "And the city had no need of the sun, neither of the moon, to shine in it, for the glory of God did lighten it, and the Lamb *is* the light thereof." In (Verse 24) it says, "And the nations of them which are saved shall walk in the light of it, and the Kings of the earth do bring their glory and honor into it." Let's, read in (Revelations 21:25) "And the gates of it shall not be shut at all by day, for there shall be no night there.

2-Heaven is a city of abundance. Many, many people have wondered about, the size of the city of God, and I know, I sure have. The Bible tells us, that it's square, and that it's approximately 1,500 miles to the East and to the West, to the North and to the South. Now, that's a lot of territory. Millions and millions of people will be there, yet no one will ever be hungry or need, anything. The Bible says, in (Revelations 7:14-17) "And I said unto Him, Sir thou knowest. And He said to me, these are they which come out of great tribulation, and have washed their robes, and made them white in the blood of the lamb." In (Verse 15) it says, "Therefore are they before the throne of God, and serve Him day and night in His temple, and He that sitteth on the throne shall dwell among them." In (Verse 16) it says, "They shall hunger no more, neither thirst anymore, neither shall the sun light on them, nor any heat." In (Verse 17) it says, "For the Lamb which is in the midst of the throne shall feed them, and shall lead them unto living fountains of waters, and God shall wipe away all tears from their eyes."

3-Heaven is a city of happiness. The people who live in this city, are very happy. They love to sing, songs of praise and thanksgiving to the Lord Jesus, for what He did for them. In Heaven there'll be no sickness, no pain, no sorrow, no sin, and no death. All these things, will be gone forever. The Bible says, in (Revelation 21:4-7) "And God shall wipe away all tears from their eyes, and there shall be no more death, neither sorrow, nor crying, neither shall there be anymore pain, for the former things are passed away." In (Verse 5) it says, "And He that sat upon the throne said, behold, I make all things new. And He said unto me, write, for these words are true and faithful." In (Verse 6) it says, "And He said unto me, it is done, I am Alpha and Omega, the beginning and the end. I will give unto Him that is athirst of the fountain of the water of life freely." In (Verse 7) it says, "He that overcometh shall inherit all things, and I will be his God, and he shall be my son." Just think, all our loves ones, who trusted in Christ, will be there. Alot, of us wonder, will we know our loved ones in Heaven? Oh yes, we will! We'll know them and we'll be with them, forever. We'll never have to say "*Goodbye*" to them again! Oh Glory! What a wonderful reunion that's going to be. One, of our greatest joys in Heaven, will be meeting those, who we led to Christ. Think of how wonderful, it'll be if someone comes up to you in Heaven and says, "Do you remember the time you talked to me about, Jesus? That was when, I realized, that I needed Him and I trusted Him as my Savior. I just want to thank you, for telling me, about the Lord Jesus, so I could be here with Him in this wonderful place forever." What a blessing, that's going to be. But, the most wonderful thing about Heaven, is this, God Himself will dwell with us. He will be our God, and we'll be His people. Nothing, will ever harm us or make us afraid.

The Bible says, in (Revelation 21:1-3) "And, I saw a new Heaven and a new earth, for the first Heaven and the first earth were passed away, and there were no more sea." In (Verse 2) it says, "And I John, saw the Holy City, New Jerusalem, coming down from God out of Heaven, prepared as a bride adorned for her husband." In (Verse 3) it says, "And I heard a great voice out of Heaven saying, behold, the tabernacle of God is with men, and He will dwell with them, and they shall be His people, and God Himself shall be with them, and be their God." Who, will be the inhabitants, of this city of our King? The ones, who will live in the beautiful city of God, are those whose names are written in the *Lambs Book Of Life*, that's those who have received the Lord Jesus, as their Saviour. In Heaven, everyone loves and worships the Lord Jesus. We'll walk the streets of Heaven, a million years and you'll never hear, anything, but words of worship and praise for Him. Since, this is true, then those who don't love the Lord Jesus, will have *No* part, in this beautiful place.

What will we do in Heaven?

1- We'll see our King face to face. The Bible says, "And they shall see His face."
2- We'll sing, a new song, of praise to the Lord Jesus, for what He did for us.
3- We will serve our King. The Bible says, "His servants shall serve Him." We don't know exactly what this service will be, but we'll enjoy it, because, we love Him.
4- We will reign with our King. The Bible says, "that we shall reign with Him for ever and ever."
5- We'll worship our King. To worship the Lord, means to adore and reverence Him because, He's worthy. Our Jesus Christ, is worthy of all worship. John, saw the throne of God in Heaven. In the midst, of that throne, he saw a lamb, as it had been slain. There's none other, than the Lord Jesus Christ.

The Lord Jesus, had many titles, but none is more wonderful than the title, *"The Lamb of God."* What does it mean, when we speak of Jesus as "Lamb of God?" It means that He died on the cross for our sins. The most precious truth in the entire Bible is this, The Son of God, loved us so much, that He left Heaven and became a man, so He could die for our sins. It's no wonder, that all in Heaven, love and worship Him. The Bible says, in (Revelation 1:5-6) "And from Jesus Christ, who is the faithful witness, and the first begotten of the dead, and the prince of the Kings of the earth. Unto,Him that loved us, and washed us from our sins in His own blood." In (Verse 6) it says, "And hath made us Kings and Priests unto God and His Father, to Him be glory and dominion for ever and ever."

People from every Tribe, Country, and Nation in the world, will gather around the throne of the Lord Jesus, to sing His praises. The Bible says, in (Revelation 5:9-10) "And they sung a new song, saying, thou art worthy to take the book, and to open the seals thereof, for thou was slain, and hast redeemed us to God by thy blood out of every kindred, and tongue, and people, and nation." In (Verse 10) it says "And hast made us unto our God Kings and Priests, and we shall reign on the earth." John, saw angles, around the throne of the Lord Jesus. The number was so great, that they couldn't be counted. They, were worshipping the Lord Jesus, in (Revelation 5:12) "Saying with a loud voice, worthy is the Lamb that was slain to receive power, and riches, and wisdom, and strength, and honour, and glory, and blessing."

Then John, describes another scene in Heaven. This time he heard *Every* creature in Heaven and earth, worshipping the Lord Jesus saying, in (Revelation 5:13) "And every creature which is in Heaven, and on the earth, and under the earth, and such as are in the seas, and all that are in them, heard I saying, blessing, and honour, and glory, and power, be unto Him that sitteth upon the throne, and unto the lamb for ever and ever." Someday with the millions, of redeemed people, will gather around the throne of the Lord Jesus, to praise and worship Him. Our King, is worthy of all worship. The King is coming! *Yes*! The King is coming! And He's coming soon. The Lord Jesus said, in (Revelation 22:12) "And, behold, I come quickly, and my reward is with me, to give every man according as his work shall be." Soon, we'll be with our King, forever.

The trials and problems, of this life will last only a short time, they'll actually, add to our *Glory* in Heaven. The Bible says, in (ll Corinthians 4:17-18) "For our light affliction, which is but for a moment, worketh for us afar more exceeding and eternal weight of Glory." In (Verse 18) it says, "While we look not at the things which are seen, but at the things which are not seen, for the things which are seen are temporal, but the things which are not seen are eternal."

The sorrows and sufferings of this world are as nothing, compared to the glory, we'll have one day. Paul the Apostle wrote, in (Romans 8:18) "For I reckon that the sufferings of this present time are *not* worthy to be *compared* with the glory which shall be revealed in us." How glorious is our future? We can't even imagine, how wonderful Heaven will be! The Bible says, in (l Corinthians 2:9) "But as it is written, Eye hath not seen, nor ear heard, neither have entered into the heart of man, the things which God hath prepared for them that love Him." May the glories of Heaven, so fill our minds, we'll be joyful, in the trials and sorrows of this life. May, Christ's love fill our hearts, that we'll live for, Him. And, may the hope of His coming so purify us, that we'll be ready when He comes. Even so, come Lord Jesus! Jesus is coming soon! We'll be with our Kng, forever!

One thing I have learned is, what you focus, on becomes reality. If we focus on Jesus Christ our Lord, He will supply us, with His power, holiness, victory, joy, strength, patience, and so much, more.

Chapter 21

❦

God, has given this wonderful Christ to us, to be everything we need. The Bible says, in (Galatians 4:6) "And because ye are sons, God hath sent forth the Spirit of His Son into your hearts, crying, Abba, Father." What does this mean? It means that Christ, is actually living in us, by His spirit. The Bible says, in (Colossians 1:27) "To whom God would make known what is the riches of the glory of this mystery amoung the Gentiles, which is Christ in you, the hope of glory." Does Christ live in every believer? *Yes, He Does*! In (ll Corinthians 13:5) the Bible says, "Examin yourselves, whether you be in the faith, prove your own selves. Know ye not your own selves, how that Jesus Christ is in you, except ye be reprobates?" In (Romans 8:9) it says, "But ye are not in the flesh, but in the Spirit, if so be that the Spirit of God dwell in you. Now, if any man have not the Spirit of Christ, he is none of His." The Bible says, we're created to be, indwelled by God, and was created "in the image of God." We're not only created in the image of God, but we're made in such a way, that God Himself could live in, us.

Here's an example, a sweater, is a piece of cloth made in the form or image of a man. It's not only, made in the image of a man, but it's made to be filled with a living person. We too, were made to be filled, with a living person, the Lord Jesus Christ, Himself!

Who is Christ? Christ lives, in the heart of every believer, but not every believer understands who Christ really is. The Gospel of John, emphasizes two great truths:

1-That Jesus Christ is God.
2-That Christ Himself is the answer to all our needs.

It'll help us to know who the great "*I Am.*" The name "*I Am*" is a name which belongs exclusively to *God.* God Himself said, "The meaning of this name, was His name."

To understand the meaning of this name, we must go back to the time, when the children of Israel, were slaves in Egypt. God chose a man named Moses, to lead his people out of Egypt and into the land, which God had promised them. Moses, was in the wilderness, tending sheep, when God appeared to him in a burning bush. The bush burned with fire, but it didn't burn up. God spoke to Moses, from the burning bush and told him to go back to Egypt, and lead the children of Israel, out of slavery and bondage. Moses, was afraid that the people wouldn't believe that God had sent him." In(Exodus 3:13-14) it says, "And

Your Way is Not God's Way

Moses said unto God, Behold, when I come unto the children of Israel, and what shall I say unto them, the God of your fathers has sent me unto you, and they shall say to me, what's His name? What shall I say unto them?" In (Verse 14) it says, "And God said unto Moses, *I Am*," THAT, "*I Am*: and He said, Thus shalt thou say unto the children of Israel, *I Am* hath sent me unto you." When God said, that His name was "*I Am*." He meant that He, is the self existent One, the God who has always existed and always will exist. It was as though God was saying, to Moses, "Moses I Am the almighty God." I'm the one who will meet all your needs. You'll need courage, to do this great work, that I have called you to do,

"*I Am*" your courage. You'll need wisdom. "*I Am*" your wisdom. You'll need strength. "*I Am*" your strength. You'll need patience. "*I Am*" your patience. "*I Am*" whatever you need. Moses, believed God, and he depended on God, to be whatever he needed, what was the result? The Bible, tells us that God brought the children of Israel out of Egypt "with a mighty hand." Christ, is the great "*I Am*." The Jews, even understood fully that the name "*I Am*" belonged only to God. *No* prophet or king, however, great he might be, would dare to use this name for himself. It's a name, which belongs exclusively to God, yet Jesus took this name for Himself. John records, Jesus astounding claim, that He is the great "*I Am*." Here, are our Lord's own words, in (John 8:24, 28, 58) it says, "I said therefore unto you, that ye shall die in your sins, for if ye believe not that "*I Am*" He, ye shall die in you sins." In (Verse 28) it says, "When

217

ye have lifted up the Son of man, then shall ye know that "*I Am*" He." In (Verse 58) it says, Verily, Verily, I say unto you, before Abraham was "*I Am*." In taking to Himself the name, "I Am" the Lord Jesus, was declaring these two great truths:

1-That He is indeed, God.
2-That He Himself, is the One who meets *All Our* needs. When Jesus took the name "*I Am*" for Himself, He was saying, in unmistakable words, that He was God.

The Jews who didn't believe in Him, hated Him, for this and they tried to kill, Him. When Jesus asked, them why they wanted to kill Him? They said, "Because you, being a man, make yourself to be God." If, Jesus wasn't really God, it would have been a terrible thing, for Him to claim to be God. But *He was*, and is, and *always will be God*. Jesus said, in (John 10:30) it says, "I and my Father are one." In (John 14:9) it says, "Jesus said unto him, have I been so long time with you, and yet hast thou not known me, Phillip? He that has seen me, has seen the Father,and how saith thy then, shew us the Father?" Jesus, is the one who meets all *Our* needs.

If we were asked, to write down a list of qualities, that we need to live a Christian life, we would probably list such things as these. We need patience, strength, wisdom, truth, victory, joy, love, peace, and we need hope. God certainly knows, that we have these needs. He, even knows about needs, that we aren't aware of, yet. How does God meet, all our needs? He meets all our needs by, giving us Christ.

The Lord Jesus, is the great "*I Am*." He's the one, who's everything we need. The Lord Jesus said, in (John 10:9) "*I Am* the door, by me if any man enter in he shall be saved, and shall go in and out, and find pasture." In (John 14:6) it says, "*I Am* the way, the truth, and the life: no man cometh unto the Father, but by me." In (John 8:12) it says, "*I Am* the light of the world: he that followeth me shall not walk in darkness, but shall have the light of life." In (John 15:1) it says, "*I Am* the true vine, and my father is the husbandman." In (John 10:14) it says, "*I Am* the good Shepard, and know my *sheep*, and am known of mine." In (John 11:25) it says, "*I Am* the resurrection, and the life: he that believeth in me, though he were dead, yet shall he live."

Jesus said, "I Am the door. He doesn't just point us to the door of Salvation, He's the door. He's not just one of the doors, He *is* the door. The only door by which we can enter, Heaven. Jesus said, "*I Am* the way." He doesn't simply show us the way to God. *He, Himself is,* the way to God, the *Only* way. If you have been saved, you have had the experience, of knowing Christ as the way to God.

Christ is our truth. Jesus said "I *Am* the truth." He doesn't simply teach us the truth, He Himself *IS* the truth. The Bible says, in (Colossians 2:3) "In whom are hid all the treasures of wisdom and knowledge."

Christ is our life. The Lord Jesus said, "*I Am* the life" Christ doesn't give us eternal life, apart from Himself. He, Himself *is* the life. If we have Christ, we have eternal life, if we don't have Him, we don't have eternal life. The Bible says, in (l John 5:12) it says, "He that hath the son have life, and he that hath not the Son of God hath not life."

Christ is our Light. Jesus said, "*I Am* 'the light of the world." Without, Christ as our light we can't "see" and understand spiritual, truth. Before, we were saved, the Bible, was a great mystery to, us. But, once Christ, came to live in us, we could see and understand spiritual truth.

Christ is our living bread. Jesus said, "I Am the living bread." Bread represents that which satisfies and sustains us.

Christ is our good Shepard. Jesus said, "*I Am* the good Shepard." We're the sheep and He is our Shepard. Just as the Shepard protects and cares for his sheep, so the Lord protects and cares for us.

Christ is our true Vine. Jesus said, "I Am the vine and you are the branches." This teaches us that our union with Christ is a Living union. Just as the living vine, supplies all that the branches needs, so shall the living Christ supply all that we need.

Christ is our resurrection. Jesus said, "I Am the resurrection." Jesus went into death and came out of it. He said, "I Am" He that lives, and was dead, and behold, "I Am alive forever, more." One day, we will have to enter into death, but because Christ is in us, we shall be raised from the dead. We'll have a new body, like Christ's glorious resurrected body. Why? Because Christ is our resurrection.

Alpha and Omega. Jesus said, "I Am the Alpha and Omega, the beginning and the ending." Found in

(Revelation1:8) it says, "I Am Alpha and Omega, the beginning and the ending, saith the Lord, which is, and which was, and which is to come, the almighty." Alpha and Omega are the first and last letters of the Greek Alphabet. Jesus is saying, "*I Am* the *first* and the *last,* the one who begins your Salvation, and the one who completes it."

"*All In All*." Christ Himself, is the answer to All our needs. He's our righteousness, joy, peace, love, patience, wisdom, holiness, victory, purity, Salvation, fullness, freedom, health, strenght, goodness, gentleness, humility, hope, life, inheritance, deliverance, resurrection, redemption, sanctification, your light, power, truth, meekness, and your "*All In All*."

Christ, lives in the heart of every believer and He's all we will ever, need. The Bible says in, (Colossians 3:11) it says "Where there is neither Greek nor Jews, circumcision nor uncircumcision, barbarian, Scythisn, bond nor free: but Christ is all, and in all." Do you need wisdom? Christ is your wisdom. Say to Him, Lord Jesus, you are my wisdom. I trust you to be my wisdom." Do you need love? Christ is your love. Say to Him, "Lord Jesus, I'm trusting you to be my love."

Do you need victory over your sins? Christ is your victory. Say to Him, "Lord Jesus, you are my victory, I'm trusting you to be my victory." God wants us to see that He has met all our needs, by giving us His Son. We, don't need to go outside of Him, for anything. Christ is the great *I Am*. God wants Him to be everything to us. The Bible says, in (Colossians 2:9-10) "For in him dwelleth all the fullness of the

God head bodily." In (Verse 10) it says, "And ye are complete in Him, which is the head of all principality and power." The Christ who lives in me is the great "*I Am*." He's my "*All And All*." Jesus Christ is our life.

For, 3 1/2 wonderful years the Lord Jesus, had walked and talked with His Disciples. As, He neared the end of His earthly ministry, Jesus spoke to them of His death, His resurrection, and His going back to the Father. Would this mean that they would be left alone? *No*! Not at all. Jesus said, in (John 14:18) "I will not leave you comfortless, I will come to you." What was Jesus saying to His disciples? He was saying, "I'm going away, but I'm coming back in a new and different way. I'm coming back in the form of the Holy Spirit. I'm coming to live in you. Just, as the Father lives in *ME*, I'm coming to live in *You*." The Lord Jesus said, in (John 14:20) "At that day ye shall know that *I AM* in my Father, and ye in me, and I in you." From our Lord's words, "you in me, and I in you," we learn that there are two aspects of our new relationship with Christ.

These can be expressed in two simple statements:

1-The believer is *In Christ*.
2-Christ is in the believer. Let's consider these two aspects of our new relationship with Christ. God has put us in Christ. This is God's fact, and it's true of every believer. The Bible says, in (Corinthians 1:30-31) "But of Him are ye in Christ Jesus, who of God is made unto

us wisdom, and righteousness, sanctification, and redemption." In (Verse 31) it says, "That, according as it is written, He that glorieth, let Him glory in the Lord."

There's no other words, in the entire Bible, more precious then these two words, "*In Christ.*" But, what does it mean to be "*In Christ?*" To be *In Christ* means, to be in union with Him. When we're born again, we become one with the Lord. The Bible says, in (I Corinthians 6:17) "But he that is joined unto the Lord is one Spirit." Because we're one with Christ, we share in all that He is and all that He has done for, us. Because, we're in Christ, we're the object of God's pleasure and delight. Just as God loves His Son and delights in Him, so He loves us and delights in us, because we're with Him. The Bible says, in (I John 4:17) "Herein is our love made perfect, that we may have boldness in the Day of Judgment, because as He is, so are we in this world."

For example, let's think of a young girl who was born into a very poor family. She's a lovely girl, but her future isn't very bright, because her family is so poor. Then, one day a wealthy man, sees her and is attracted to her. In time, he falls in love with her and asks her to be his bride. At the moment, these two are joined in marriage, this young girl is no longer poor. She is joined in marriage, to a wealthy man and she'll shares in all that he is and all that he has.

It's the same with Christ. Because we're joined to Christ, we share in all that He is, and all that He has done for us. How can we be sure that we're "*In*

Christ." We can be sure because, the Bible, declares that it's, so. It was God, who put us, in Christ and it's God who tells us, that He has done this. The Bible says, in (ll Corinthians 1:21) "Now, He which establisheth us with you in Christ, and hath anointed us, is *God.*" Our being In Christ, in union with Him, isn't something we have done. Oh No! It's something God, has done for us. Our part is to see it, believe it, and rejoice in it.

Chapter 22

❦

Christ is in the believer. Now, because we're "*In Christ*" in union with Him, we have a perfect standing before God. But what about our life here on earth? We want to live a life that is pleasing to God, but, by ourselves, we're unable to do it. We want to do what is right and good, but it seems that the more we struggle to live right, the more we fail. The Apostle Paul, had this same problem. He wrote, in (Romans 7:19) "For the good that I would I do not, but the evil which I would not, that I do." No matter how hard Paul tried, he couldn't live the way he wanted, to. Paul says, in (Romans7:18) "For I know that in me (that is, in my flesh,) dwelleth no good thing, for to will is present with me, but how to perform that which is good I find not."

Christians down through the years have had the same experience, that Paul had. We want to do what's right and good, but we're unable to do it. How, does God solve this problem? He solves this problem, by giving Christ to live in us. The Bible says, in (Galatians 4:6) "Because ye are sons, God hath sent the Spirit of His Son, into your hearts, crying, Abba, Father." We know, that Christ is living in us, because of God's clear statements, that the living Christ is dwelling in us. In (Galatians 2:20) it says,"I am crucified with Christ, nevertheless I live, yet not I, but Christ liveth in me, and the life which I now live in the flesh I live by the faith of the Son of God, who loved me, and gave Himself for me."

In (Colossians 1:27) Paul says,"To whom God would make known what is the riches of the glory of this mystery among the Gentiles, which is Christ in you, the hope of glory." Again and again in His word, God seeks to empress on us the great *Truth* that the living Christ is dwelling in everyone of His children. In (ll Corinthians 13:5) Paul wrote, "Examine yourselves, whether ye be in the faith, prove your own selves. Know ye not your own selves, how that Jesus Christ is in you, except ye be reprobates?" In (Ephesians 3:17) Paul, prayed for the believers, saying, "That Christ may dwell in your hearts by faith, that ye, being rooted and grounded in love."

Sometimes, a Christian will look for some special feeling or emotion before, he'll believe that Christ is living in his heart. But God, plainly tells us that Christ, lives in the hearts of every child of His. What God says, in His Word, is true regardless of our feelings. Accept God's clear statements, that the living Christ, is living in you. Believe it's true, because God says, it's true. Christ is *All* we need, Christ is the answer to our every need. He's indeed our "*All In All*."

You may think, how do I experience all these things, that Christ is to me? We experience them as we abide in Christ. Jesus said, "abide in *Me*, and I in you." Our part is to abide in Him. His part, is to be everything that we need. What does it mean, to abide in Christ? God has put us, *in* Christ and He wants us to abide in Him. We're never told to get into Christ, for we're already in Christ. But, the Lord Jesus says to us, in (John 15:4) "Abide in me, and I in you. As the branch cannot bear fruit of itself, except It abide in the vine, no more can ye, except ye abide in me." In (John 15:5) it says, "*I Am* the vine, ye are the branches, He that abideth in me, and I in him, the same bringeth forth much fruit, for without me ye can do nothing."

The word "abide" means "to stay." If you go to your home and abide there, it means that you stay there. When you abide in your home, everything in that home is available to you, the lights, heating, furniture, and the food, everything. When you abide in Christ, all that's in Christ is available to you. His love, strength, patience, holiness, and His wisdom, everything. What does it mean to "abide in Christ?" It, means to remain in unbroken fellowship with Him. How do we abide in Him? We abide in Him, by recognizing His presence in us, obeying Him and drawing on Him for all our needs. What breaks our abiding in Christ? *Sin*! When we sin, our abiding in the Lord is broken. As soon, as we confess that "Sin" to the Lord, our fellowship with Him, is restored. Once again, we are abiding in Him, what a mighty God we have.

A great man of God, once explained to his little boy of six years old. What it meant to "abide in Christ." His six year old boy, had received Christ as his Savior, when he was six, and his father, wanted him, to understand the truth of "abiding in Christ." Calling his son into his office, his father took a card and drew a circle. Inside, the circle, he listed all of the things Christ is to us. Putting the point of his pencil in the center of the circle, he said, "there son, you see that pencil? I want you, to keep in Christ, as the pencil is in the circle. Inside, you'll find everything, to make you happy and obedient. But, there's a lot of little doors all around the circle. It's, when you go out of one of these doors, that you are being disobedient." Then, he drew little doors, leading out from the circle. These doors represented, the sins that take us from abiding in Christ. The little boy was so happy to understand this. So, he told others, in his own words what he had just learned. He carried, the card around, so he could show, what it meant to abide in Christ, and how he was staying, in the center of the circle. Then, one day, the little boy, went to his father, crying. When his father asked, "why," he was crying. His son said, "I have gone outside of the circle!" The boys *fear,* was that he couldn't get back inside the circle. His father, kneeled down with his son and they looked at the card together. The father said, "now, son, tell me what door you went out of?" The boy, showed it to his father, "well," said the father, "the way to get back inside again, is to enter by the same door you went out of. The way to do this, is to confess the sin to God. The moment we do this,

Your Way is Not God's Way

God forgives us, and we come back into the circle and once again, we're abiding in Christ. How, happy the little boy was to learn this! This is a very simple story, but it does explain what I meant by, to "abide in" Christ. As we, recognize Christ's presence in us, obey Him, and draw upon Him for our needs, we abide in Him, and enjoy His love and fellowship. If we sin, we should confess that to God, immediately.

One of the great secrets, of a Christian life, is to turn to God immediately, when we fail. Satan, always tries to keep us, from doing this, but God wants us, to confess our sins to Him. The moment we do this, God forgives us, and we are once again abiding in Christ. It's very simple if, we sin, we confess the sin, and we live by Christ. The Lord Jesus said, "I live by the Father." What was Jesus saying? He was saying, "The Father lives in me," and I live by Him, I recognize His presence in me, I obey Him, always, I draw upon Him, for all that I need. Just as Christ, lived by the Father, who dwelled in Him, so we're to live by Christ who dwells in us.

The Bible says, that Christ is "our life." When the Apostle Paul, realized that Christ was his life, he no longer had to say, "how do I perform that which is good. Instead, he said triumphantly, in (Philippians 4:13) "I can do all things through Christ which strengtheneth me."

There's three things, we need to do, beginning right now:

1-Recognize Christ's presence in you. Say to yourself, Christ lives in me. Christ, does live in you. Believe, that He's there, and begin to act accordingly, and God will make it real to you. When the Devil, knocks at the door of my heart, I just say, "Lord Jesus," the devil, bows down and says, "I see that I have come, to the wrong place" and he leaves, simply recognizing Christ's presence in your heart, and trusting Him, to be your victory over temptation. This is just what we must do.

2-Obey Him at all times. We can't enjoy, this wonderful indwelling Christ, if He's not loved, honored and obeyed. We must be ready always to say, "Lord Jesus, I will please you," even through, it may mean displeasing to everyone, else.

3-Draw upon Him for all your needs. Whatever you need, take Christ as that need. Remember He's the great "*I Am.*" Take Him as your victory, let Him overcome temptation for you. He'll not fail you. Abiding in Christ, is simply giving, oneself to the Lord Jesus, the great "*I Am*" trusting Him to keep us and letting Him do, all for us. As we abide in Christ, He makes Himself real to us. He becomes the great "*I Am*" to us. Whatever, we need, He becomes that very thing to us. Day by day, as we learn to abide in Christ and to trust Him, to be everything we need, we are being changed. The Bible says, that we're being "conformed to the image of God's Son." This means, that we're becoming more and more like, Jesus. One day, we shall see Jesus, face to face, and we shall be like Him, in every way. The Christian life, is Christ, living His life in us.

Chapter 23

❧

Dealing with anger. Now this is something, that I have to get real deep, into the Bible with. Anger, we all have it. How do we deal with it? The Lord led me to these verses, in (James 1:19-20) it says, "Wherefore, my beloved brethren, let every man be swift to hear, slow to speak, slow to wrath." In(Verse 20) it says, "For the wrath of man worketh not the righteousness of God." When, we became a Christian, our conduct and personality, should undergo certain changes. One, of these changes has to do with, temper. A Christian should react in a Christian way. We shouldn't lose our tempers. We'll deal with the problem, of anger and temper. We'll see the *Root* cause, of temper and learn how, we can be delivered from the sin of having a bad temper.

The destructiveness of anger. The first man, to discover the destructive power of anger was, Cain. Cain and his brother, Abel, were the first two sons of Adam. When these sons grew up, Cain became a farmer and Abel became a Sheppard. Cain and Abel had been taught the right way to worship, God. They knew that God, required an offering of innocent animals, as a sacrifice for their sins. But, when they came to worship God, only one brother was obedient to God. Abel, brought a lamb, as his offering, but Cain brought fruit, from his crops, as his offering. God, accepted Abel and his offering, but he, rejected Cain's, offering. As a result of this, Cain, became very angry. He was angry at God and jealous of his brother. God warned Cain, of the consequences of his anger. God's message to Cain was this "look out!" Our anger, is like a roaring lion, laying in wait, outside your door. You, must master your anger or it will master you. But Cain, didn't respond to God's warning, his jealousy of Abel, turned into hatred. One day, as Cain and Abel were in the field together, Cain, rose up against his brother and murdered him. So, the first man born, into this world, became a murderer, because he didn't control his anger.

Dealing with anger. Like Cain, we have the "lion" of anger within, us. We must master it or it will master, us. God, hasn't said, that we're never to be angry, but He has warned us, of the danger of uncontrolled anger. The Bible says, in (Ephesians 4:26) "Be ye angry, and sin not, let not the sun go down upon your wrath." Anger, is the most violent of human emotions. Because, it involves such strong feelings, anger borders closely to sin. The Bible, doesn't say, "be kind, but sin not" or "love, but do not sin," because kindness and love are far removed from sin. But when we're angry, we're in danger of sinning. I have always said, "if we're to be angry and sin not, we must be angry at nothing, but sin."

There's three things, we can do with our anger:

1- We can express it. When anger is out of control, it will do alot of damage. When, we become so angry, that we want to lash out at someone and hurt them, we are sinning. We, call this "losing our tempers." Sometimes, we think, that we show how strong we are, when we lose our tempers, but losing our temper is a sign of weakness, not strength. The Bible says, in (Ecclesiastes 7:9) "Be not hasty in thy spirit to be angry, for anger resteth in the bosom of fools."

2- We can suppress it. To suppress anger, is to keep it inside. Some, people lose their tempers and express their anger openly. Others have the same angry feelings, but manage to keep them bottled up. Inside anger, that's bottled up, or kept inside of us, hurts and keeps on hurting. It turns to resentment and bitterness, and it can bring on depression, as well as many different kinds of physical illnesses.

3- We can confess it. The best way to handle angry feelings, is to tell God about them. This is a very good way to "let off steam" without sinning. God knows us better, than we know ourselves, and we'll always find Him, to be understanding. Tell God about your angry feelings. Just being in God's presence, helps to calm us. It also helps us, to see things in their proper perspective. So, many times, we discover that the things, we're disturbed about wasn't really so important, after all.

We, must deal with the sin of temper. Temper is uncontrolled anger. It's always wrong. When we lose our temper, there's only one thing to do. We, must confess it to God, as sin and claim the cleansing blood of Christ. If we've offended or hurt others, we must, of course, apologize. If we don't, then it becomes a sin. Regardless of how many times you lose your temper, you must make things right with others, each time. This will humble you and help you, to see the damage done by your temper. It's best not to go to the other person, while you are still upset, but after you have calmed down, then go and make things right. We, must deal with the cause of temper. Even though, we faithfully confess our sins to God everytime we lose our tempers, we still have a problem. The problem is, that we keep doing the same things, over and over again. We lose our tempers, and we confess it. Then, we lose our tempers again and confess it again. We do the samething over and over. No matter how hard we try, we continue to lose our tempers.

Is there a remedy for this problem? *Yes, There Is!* The first thing we must do, is to discover what caused, us to lose our temper. The Bible, doesn't say much about temper. The reason is, that the Bible, is concerned with the *Root* cause of temper, not just with the temper itself. What's the root cause of temper? It is *Self*! Temper is produced by self. When ever temper is expressed on the outside, we may be sure, that there's an angry self on the inside. We may try to control our temper, but unless self is dealt with, we will continue to get angry and lose our temper.

Now, let's look at a few temper producing situations, so that we may see more clearly, that self is the cause of tempers:

1-Someone puts us down. Being "put down" or belittled by others, is one of the most common causes, of losing our temper. Someone, says something, unkind or hurtful, about us and we become angry on the inside. Our self pride is injured. This is, one of many forms of self. There's self pity, self love, jealousy, self will, self exaltation, self justification, and self righteousness, just to name a few.

2-We can't have our own way. We're self-willed and determined to have our own way. When, someone crosses us and we can't have our way, we may sulk or pout, or flare up with anger. What's the root cause of this? It's *Self.*

3-Someone is honored above us. We, like to be looked up to and admired by others. For this reason, we're jealous of others, when they succeed. Jealousy, often turns into anger, when someone gets the job, or honor that we wanted. Again, the root cause of these wrong feelings, is self. These are, a few temper-producing situations, but they show us, that the root cause of temper, is self. We may not realize it, but the main reason for all our discontent, is that we love ourselves and want to please, ourselves. As long, as we make ourselves, the center of everything, we'll react with anger when anyone crosses us.

To sum this up, temper comes from within us. It comes from self. Until the problem of self is dealt with, the problem of temper will not be solved. Now, read his carefully, there's a self, which I'm to accept and a self which I'm to deny. I'm to accept myself as the special, unique person, which God created me to be. But I'm to deny self, that sinful self-life, which is a form of the flesh. Because self, is so hateful to God and so destructive to us, God did something about it. What did God do about self? God dealt with self, by putting us in Christ, on the cross. Thank God, for doing this. When Christ, was crucified we were crucified with him. Why did God crucify us with Christ? He crucified us, with Christ so that we, may no longer be *Ruled By Self.*

The Bible says, in (Romans 6:6) "Knowing this, that our old man is crucified with Him, that the body of sin might be destroyed, that henceforth, we should not serve sin." In (Corinthians 1:30-31) it says, "But of Him are ye in Christ Jesus, who of God is made unto us wisdom, and righteousness, and sanctification, and redemption." In (Verse 31) it says, "That, according as it is written, He that glorieth, let him glory in the Lord."

Two great facts which are true of every Christian:

1-Christ died for us.
2-We died with Christ. The whole great truths concerning our union, with Christ in His death, burial, and resurrection are fully covered. An understanding of these truths, are absolutely essential to a life of victory. God wants us to see that, in Christ, we died to our old life. We're not the same person we were, before. We're "a new creation" *In Christ*. We don't have to give in to our old sins. We died to all our sins, including the sin of temper. The Bible says, in (Romans 6:2) "God forbid. How shall we, that are dead to sin, live any longer therein?"

Now there are some practical steps we must take:

1-We must see our need. Many people, when angry, simply will *not* admit their anger. They say, "I am not angry!" Others, admit that they have a temper, but don't see it, as a serious sin. Actually, temper is one of the worst sins.

The Bible, lists uncontrolled anger, along with such sins, in (Galatians 5:19-21) "Now the works of the flesh are manifest, which are these, adultery, fornication, uncleanlyness, lasciviousness." In (Verse 20) it says, "Idolatry witch craft, hatred, variance, emulations, wrath, strife, seditions, heresies." In (Verse 21) it says, "Envyings, murders, drunkenness, reveling, and such like: of the which I tell you before, as I have also told you in time past, that they which do such things shall not inherit the kingdom of God." Temper, is simply not acceptable in the life of a Christian." In (Ephesians 4:31-32) it says, "Let all bitterness, and wrath, and anger, and clamor, and evil speaking, be put away from you, with all malice." In (Verse 32) it says, "And be ye kind one to another, tender hearted, forgiving one another, even as God for Christ sake hath forgiven you." Unless we see the seriousness, of our temper and determine to be delivered from it. *We Will Not Overcome It.* If we're satisfied to go on as we have been going, we'll know nothing of *God's* victory, over the sin of temper.

- 2-We must accept responsibility for our temper. It's very easy to excuse ourselves, by blaming someone else, for our temper. We say, "if so and so hadn't spoken to me like that, I wouldn't have lost my temper." Then, in other words, we think that our temper is an *External* problem, that it's caused by something from outside. The real true fact, is that our temper is an *Internal* problem. Temper, comes from within us, not from outside. Others, may say or *Do* things that irritate us, but no one can make us lose our *Temper Except Ourselves.*
- 3-We, must count on our death with Christ. God, has told us plainly, that He has delivered us from the power of sin, and self, by our death with Christ. God tells us, to count on these great facts. The Bible says, in (Romans 6:11-12) "Likewise reckon ye also yourselves to be dead indeed unto sin, but alive unto God

through Jesus Christ our Lord." In (Verse 12) it says, "Let not sin therefore reign in your mortal body, that ye should obey it in the lusts thereof." We must put God's truth into practice. When we find ourselves getting angry, we can say, "Hold on! I'm not acing like the person I really am. I'm not the person I used to be." Like I always tell, people, "Who I was then, isn't who I am today." My old angry self, was crucified with Christ. I don't have to give in to my temper, anymore. I'm a new creature in Christ. Christ lives in me. He's my life.

4- We must deny self. Whether or not we lose our temper, isn't determined by, what happens on the outside. It's determined by the one, in control on the inside.

Christ alone has the *Right* to rule in our life, but self will still try to rule. Every Christian, must choose, whether he'll be ruled by *Christ* or by *Self*. It's God's, purpose that Christ reign on the throne of our heart. In order for Him to reign, self must be kept in the place of death on the cross. It's one thing to understand the teaching, that we're crucified with Christ. It's another thing, to put it into practice and actually deny self. But, that's what we must do. Jesus said, in (Luke 9:23-24) "If any man will come after me, let him deny himself, and take up his cross daily, and follow me." In (Verse 24) it says, "For whosoever will save his life shall lose it, but whosoever will lose his life for my sake, the same shall save it."

To overcome temper, we must deny self. What does it mean to "deny self?" To deny self means to choose God's will, instead of our own will. Denying self is saying, "I don't have to have my own way. I fully accept God's way." The world says, "look out for yourself," but Jesus says, "deny yourself." We'll never control our temper, until we give up our way and *Choose God's Way*. We'll find that the Lord, will allow us, to be in many situations where we're mistreated or inconvenienced. This is God's way, of dealing with our self- life and our temper.

God's, purpose in all these situations is that, we learn to be patient and denying self gladly, letting God have His way in our life. When, someone keeps you waiting a long time, you don't have to lose your temper. You may say, "Lord, you know that I need to learn patience." You're in control of my circumstances, and you have allowed this, to teach me to be more patient. Measure a man by what it takes to make him angry. When someone says or does something that hurts your pride, you don't have to get angry. You can say, "Lord, you know how proud I am, I thank you, for dealing with me about my sinful pride." When others do don't what you want them to do and you can't have your own way, this is your chance to die to self. You can say, "Lord, I always want to have my own way, but you know what is best for me. I fully accept your way." In, whatever situation the Lord arranges for us, we can say, "Lord this is what you have arranged for me." This is your way of dealing with my self-life and my temper. I accept this from you and thank you, for it." The root cause of temper is *Self.* God crucified me with Christ, that I'll be delivered from my sinful temper.

Reaction and Resentment. In (Psalms 119:164-165) it says, "Seven times a day do I praise thee, because of thy righteous judgments." In (Verse 165) it says, "Great peace have they which love thy law, and nothing shall offend them." Our response to what someone says or does, is called a reaction. For example, someone says something, nice about us and we feel good. Feeling good is our reaction. Someone says something about us that is not true and we get angry. Getting angry is also a reaction. We may have never, thought much about reactions, but actually they're tremendously important. We'll see why they're so important and gain some insight, that will help us with our reactions.

The reason our reactions, are so important, is that they can have long term and even eternal consequences. What happens to us is'nt as important as our reactions to it. The thing that troubles us, will pass in time, but our reactions can have eternal consequences.

The story of Joseph, in the Old Testament, can teach us so much about reactions. Joseph, was next to the youngest of Jacobs's twelve sons. He was especially loved by his father. Because of this, his brothers were jealous of him and hated him. One day, Joseph told his brothers, about a dream God had given him. He said to his brothers, in effect, "I had a dream, in which God showed me, that one day I would rule over you, and that you would bow down to me." This made his brothers hate him even more.

When the opportunity came, Joseph's brothers, sold him as a slave into Egypt. Through no fault of his own, he was falsely accused, of attempting to seduce his masters wife, Joseph spent years in prison, for a crime he didn't commit. In all this, Joseph, didn't become bitter or resentful. In time, God exalted Joseph. Under Pharaoh, Joseph became ruler over all of Egypt. Through wisdom, given to him by God, Joseph stored grain, during seven years of plentiful crops. Then came a great famine, over all the earth. During this time, Joseph's brothers came to Egypt, seeking food for themselves and their families. They, stood before Joseph, but did'nt recognize him. As prime minister of Egypt. Joseph could have used his power, to get even with his brothers. He could've said, "now I have my brother's right where I want them. I'm going to make them pay for their sins. I'll let them know that the dream, I had about my being exalted, over them was really true. I'm going to show them, that they can't do, what they did to me and get away with it." Apparently, no such thoughts of vengeance crossed Joseph mind. He said, to his brothers, "be not grieved nor angry with yourselves, that ye sold me hither, for God did send me before you to preserve life, so now, it was not you, that sent me hither, but God." Joseph, allowed God to be in control of his reactions. He was kind and gracious to his brothers. He took good care of them and their families.

Joseph's reactions, were the right reactions, and they had eternal consequences for good. Dealing with our life situations, we may not have as difficult, of a

Your Way is Not God's Way

situation as Joseph faced, but we're sure to receive some mistreatment. Living in a world of sinful, rebellious human beings, we shouldn't be surprised, at any unkind or unfair treatment we receive. Though, such treatment may trouble us at the time, it needs not have any lasting effect on our life. What is, important is our reactions. They do have, a lasting effect upon our life and the lives of others.

Now, let's look at some situations, that usually cause us to react, in the wrong way and see how we can handle them in the *Right Way*. In, each instance, *Note,* that the person was able to choose his/ her reactions:

1-Rudeness or discourtesy. *No*, one likes rude or discourteous treatment. Our usual response, to such treatment, is to act the same way the other person has acted. This kind of reaction, is displeasing to God. The Bible says, that "Christians are to be courteous." For example, I walked the other night with my friend, to a nearby news stand. He bought a paper, thanked the newsboy politely. The newsboy didn't even look up or acknowledge him. A sullen fellow isn't he? I commented. "Oh, he's that way every night," replied my friend. "Then why, do you continue to be so polite to him, I asked?" "Why not, replied my friend?" "Why, should I let him decide how I'm going to act?"

2-Unfair treatment. Almost everyone, receives unfair treatment, at some time or other. This can cause us pain and distress. Being a Christian doesn't mean, that we're insensible to the way we're treated. But, as Christians, we can choose what our reaction will be. For example, the daughter of a high school principle received an unfair detention. She could've created a big scene about it, or she could've held resentment in her heart. But, she did neither. She simply dismissed it by saying, "oh well, I've done a lot of things for which I should have gotten detentions for, and I didn't. So, this isn't so bad." Happy is the Christian, who can handle unfair treatment, as well as this girl, did.

3-Hurt Pride. When, someone says something about you, that hurts your pride, you can react angrily. You can carry that hurt and resentment around for, the rest of your life. How much better, it would be, if you could say, with a big heart, "so and so, hurt my pride, by what they said, but it wasn't nearly as bad, as what they could've said. If they only knew me as I know myself, they could've said, ten times as much and still be telling the truth."

4-Offenses. It's easy to become angry and react wrong, when others commit offenses, against us, but let's remember that, *We Will Reap What We Sow*. God will deal with us, according to the way we deal with others. If we're kind and forgiving with them, God will be gracious and forgiving with us. If we're hard and unforgiving with others, God will be as unforgiving with us. Jesus said, in (Matthew 6:14-15) "For if ye forgive men their trespasses, your Heavenly

Father will also forgive you." In (Verse 15) it says, "But if ye forgive not men their trespasses, neither will your Father forgive your trespasses." It reminds me; I'm a very outspoken person. When someone asks, for my opinion on something, I honestly give them my answer. On one occasion, a co- worker came to me, very angry, about something that had happened to him at work, and I told him to calm down and forgive them. He proudly says, to me "*I Never Forgive*." I turned to him and said, "then I hope my friend, that you never sin."

5-Jumped on by someone. When, someone makes an angry or harsh remark to us, we feel like replying, in a like manner. This will only make a bad situation, worse. It's better, if we have control of ourselves and handle the situation with a soft answer. For example, at a round table discussion, things became so heated, that a woman flared up at the leader and said, "I want you to know, that I absolutely disagree with, you." The leader turned toward the woman, paused a moment, and with a friendly smile said, "I like you, too!" He had control of himself. The tension was broken. The atmosphere was relieved. Later, as he went out, after the meeting, the woman turned to him with a smile and said, "I like you too!" How wise this man was. How wise we'll be to have such control, over ourselves when we are jumped on. The Bible says, in (Proverbs 15:1-4) "A soft answer turneth away wrath, but grievous words stir up anger." In (Verse 2) it says, "The tongue of the wise useth knowledge aright, but the mouth of fools poureth out foolishness." In (Verse 3) it says, "The eyes of the Lord are in every place, beholding the evil and the good." In (Verse 4) it says, "A wholesome tongue is a tree of life, but perverseness therein is a breach in the spirit."

6-Criticism. Criticism is either *True* or it's *False*. If it's true, we need to learn from it. If it's false, we shouldn't let it disturb us. I've always said, "if you don't believe the truth, then you will believe a lie." Simple as that, we can leave the matter with God, knowing that He will take care of it. I believe this whole heartily. When you're in the right, you can afford to keep your temper. When you're in the wrong, you can't afford to lose it.

7-Mistakes. Everyone makes mistakes at one time or another. Often, we try to excuse ourselves or blame somebody else for our mistakes. A wrong reaction, added to a mistake, makes the matter, that much worse. On the other hand, if we admit our mistakes and apologize correctly, God can use, even our mistakes to His glory.

The true fact is, there's no situation, in which anger, is our only possible response. We don't have to lose our temper. Others, may say or do things that irritate us, but no one can make us lose our temper. If I get angry and lose my temper, it's because I choose to do so. I can choose to respond with patients, humor, kindness, forgiveness, or in some other Godly way. Beware of holding on to the wrong reactions. The dangers of a wrong reaction is holding on to them, until they develop into deeper problems.

When we hold on to wrong reactions, it becomes a serious case of resentment. If resentment is harbored, it will become bitterness. Resentment and bitterness can and will destroy us. Now, let's consider some things, we should do to prevent resentment and bitterness, from getting a foothold on our lifes:

1-Overlook of offenses. Believers, should stay in constant fellowship with God, through prayer, and the reading of His Word. When we're in fellowship with God, we're able to overlook many things, that otherwise might offend us. The Bible says, in (Psalms 119:165) "Great peace have they which love thy law, and nothing shall offend them." It's to our credit, when we restrain our anger and overlook insults. The Bible says, in (Proverbs 19:11-12) "The discretion of a man deferreth his anger, and it is his glory to pass over a transgression." In (Verse 12) it says, "The king's wrath is as the roaring of a lion, but his favours is as dew upon the grass."

2-Clear up misunderstandings promptly. One of Satan's devices, is to promote misunderstandings, between God's children. He, injects a bit of deception and falsehood into a situation. The result, is that people hold things against others, which they may have never been guilty of.

The Bible insists, that when we have a misunderstanding with another believer, we go to him and make things right. If God's children, obeyed the Lord in this, many problems among us would be eliminated. Here's a very good example. A missionary leader, was conducting a conference among missionaries, in a foreign land. One day, a missionary came to him and said, "one of the missionaries here has something against me and I don't know why." Soon thereafter, another missionary came to see the leader and said, the very same thing, about the first one. As it turns out, each one thought that the other, had something against each other. Both were wrong. There was really nothing wrong between them, but Satan, had put the thought into their minds and they had accepted it and were deceived.

3-Reject wrong attitudes quickly. Sometimes, we may not be able to control our instant reaction in a given situation, but we can, prevent a wrong reaction, from becoming a resentment. We can choose to reject a wrong attitude. God's Word says, "Let not the sun go down upon your wrath, neither give place to the Devil." God, is telling us here, that we're not to hold on to wrong attitudes.

4-Pray for the other person. Any time, we sense that we may be holding a bad attitude toward someone, we should be praying for them. Even though that person, may have mistreated you, pray for them each and every day. Pray for yourself, that God, may keep you from resentment. Jesus said, "Pray for them which despitefully use you." God will help us, in these areas, for He loves helping us.

Our reactions must be under Christ's control. Our reactions aren't determined by what happens to us on the outside, they're determined, by the one who is in control of the inside. If self is in control, we'll react according to self, if Christ is in control, we'll react according to his life.

As God's children, we don't have the liberty, to react as we please. Our reactions, must be under Christ's control. God, has given Christians definite commands, as to how they are to react. The Bible says, in (I Thessalonians 5:14-18) "Now we exhort you, brethren, warn them that are unruly, comfort the feeble minded, support the weak, be patient toward all men." In (Verse 15) it says, "See that none render evil for evil unto any man, but ever follow that which is good, both among yourselves, and to all men." In (Verse 16) it says, "Rejoice evermore." In (Verse17) it says, "Pray without ceasing." In (Verse 18) it says, "In ever thing give thanks, for this is the will of God in Christ Jesus concerning you."

In that three letter word "see" lies our responsibility. We're to see to it, that we don't render evil for evil. This means, that we're not going to get even with people, but rather suffer mistreatment patiently. Our Lord Jesus Himself, is our example. The Bible says, in (I Peter 2:18-25) "Servants, be subject to your master with all fear, not only to the good and gentle, but also to the froward." In (Verse 19) it says, "For this is thankworthy if a man for conscience toward God endure grief, suffering wrongfully." In (Verse 20) it says, "For what glory is it, if, when ye be buffeted for your faults, ye shall take it patiently? But if, when ye do well, and suffer for it, ye take it patiently, this is acceptable with God." In (Verse 21) it says, "For even hereunto were ye called, because Christ also suffered for us, leaving us an example, that ye should follow His steps." In (Verse 22) it says, "Who did no sin, neither was guile found in his mouth." In (Verse 23) it says, "Who, when he was reviled, reviled not again, when he suffered, he threatened not, but committed himself to Him that judgeth righteously." In (Verse 24) it says, "Who His own self bare our sins in His own body on the tree, that we, being dead to sin, should live unto righteousness, by whose stripes we were healed." In (Verse 25) it says, "For ye were as sheep going astray, but are now returned unto the Shepard and Bishop of your souls." God wants us to see the importance of our reactions.

I like to think of our reactions like this. The eternal substance, of us living, is never in the thing itself, but in the quality of our reactions toward it. If in hard times, we're kept from resentment, held in silence and filled with sweetness, that's what matters. The event that distressed us, will pass from memory, as a wind, that passed and is gone. But, what they were, while the wind was blowing, has eternal consequences. So therefore, it matters little, what happens to us. The important thing that really matters, is how we react to what happens. May the Lord help and enable us, to see that our reactions have eternal consequence. The things that trouble us, will pass in time, but our reactions have eternal consequences.

In the Bible, let's look in (Ephesians 4:23-32) "And be renewed in the sprit of your mind." In (Verse 24) it says, "And that ye put on the new man, which after God is created in righteousness and true holiness." In (Verse 25) it says, "Wherefore putting away lying, speak ever man truth with his neighbor, for we are member one of another." In (Verse 26) it says, "Be ye angry, and sin not, let not the sun go down on your wrath." In (Verse 27) it says, "Neither give place to the Devil." In (Verse 28) it says, "Let him that stole steal no more, but rather let him labor, working with his hands the things which are good, that he may have to give to him that needeth." In (Verse 29) it says, "Let no corrupt communication proceed out of your mouth, but that which is good to the use of edifying, that it may minister grace unto the hearers." In (Verse 30) it says, "And grieve not the Holy Spirit of God, whereby ye are sealed unto the day of redemption." In (Verse 31) it says, "Let all bitterness, and wrath, and anger, and clamor, and evil speaking, be put away from you, with all malice." In (Verse 32) it says, "And be ye kind one to another, tenderhearted, forgiving one another, even as God for Christ's sake hath forgiven you."

Chapter 24

What is resentment? Why is it so destructive? What effect will it have on us? How can we turn from bitterness to forgiveness? Resentment, is that deep feeling of displeasure or anger, that we have toward someone because of a past offence. It's our painful memory of past hurts. Resentment, is the one great enemy, of good and right relationships. It'll destroy friendships and turn friends into enemies. But the most damaging effect of resentment, is the total destruction of the person, who's willing to hold on to it. Of all of Satan's evils, one of the most destructive things, that can happen to us, is holding on to resentment, it's the worst. It's like a deadly germ, working constantly to gain power over us, to destroy us. No right thinking person, would harbor and nourish a deadly germ in there body, knowing that this germ would eventually kill them. Yet, many people hold on to the sin of resentment, which is far more destructive than any germ.

Seeing that resentment is such a deadly sin, we might as well ask ourselves, "why do we hold on to resentment?" There's a number of reasons, some of them are:

1- We feel justified in our resentment. The reason why it's difficult for us to recognize the poisonous nature of resentment, is that it seems okay or right to us. We feel that we're justified in our resentment. We often say, to ourselves, "It's only human or natural to resent so and so." In order for us, to justify our resentment, we often build up in our mind, a false image of the, other person. We push aside, the whole picture of what that person is and all the good and decent things he/she may have done, and focus on there offenses against us.

2- It makes us feel superior. When, someone does something that offends or hurts us, we take a superior attitude toward that person. We say, to ourselves, "why I would never do a thing like that!" We like this feeling of superiority and therefore we hold on tight to our resentment.

3- We like to keep score. Sometimes, we hold on to our resentments in order, to have something to offset our future offenses, we may commit. We want to be able to say, "maybe I was wrong in that matter. But, you did such and such to me, for I remember it." So, don't keep score.

4- We enjoy our resentments. Strange as it may seem, we keep our hurts alive, for the pleasures we can get out of them. We, enjoy nursing our wounds and feeling sorry for ourselves, after someone has offended us.

One thing I do know, is resentment grows into bitterness, completely the Devils work. Resentment, is one of the most unusual of all sins, that it's meant to punish the other person, yet it's far more hurtful to us, than it could ever be to the other person. Sometimes, the other person may not even be aware of having done anything wrong at all. Our resentment doesn't harm them at all, but it's very destructive to us. If, we hold on to resentment, it can and will grow into bitterness. Bitterness affects our health, mind, personality and relationship with God.

Let's consider these four areas of our lifes:

1-Bitterness affects our health. Bitterness is a poison to our body. Resentment, bitterness, hatred and unforgiveness can cause ulcers, high blood pressure, and dozens of other diseases. It has been estimated by some doctors, that as much as 90% of all our illnesses are caused from, anger, fear, resentment, and bitterness. That's so unbelievable, but so very true and it gets worse. Holding bitterness in your heart, can cause you to lose sleep and to be tired most of the time. It"ll take away the enjoyment of your food. It'll steal your happiness. In time, it"ll show in your eyes and on your face. Hatred makes you a slave, to the person you hate. A friend told me once, that the moment he started hating a man, he become his slave. He said, "I can't enjoy my work anymore, because he controls my thoughts. My resentments, produce too many stress hormones, in my body and I become tired, after only a few hours of work. The work, I formerly enjoyed is now, a drudgery. Even my vacations, cease to give me pleasures, I can't escape his grasp on my mind." I simply said to him, "go to God, and place all that hatred, resentment and bitterness, at the Lord's feet. And, get forgiveness, back into your heart and life. Just let God fully take care of it." The Lord loves us and doesn't want his people suffering.

2-Bitterness affects our mind. I say this because, I was in a deep depression. It got to where I couldn't handle it any longer. I prayed to God in Heaven, to take it all away. In a snap it was completely gone. That's how powerful our God is. Right then, the depression was, gone. An, experience, I'll never forget. Our God, is very alive and is willing to heal His people. Oh! Thank you, Lord! It has been proven that bitterness can, and does bring on depression. People who have a tendency to be depressed, much of the time, are often people, who hold resentment against a loved one or relative, who hurt them earlier in life. If you're one of these people, you'll never know the lasting *Victory* over depression, until you get rid of that bitterness. And the only way out of this is through Jesus Christ our Lord.

3-Bitterness affects our personality. The more we resent someone, the more we think about them. And the more we think about a person, the more we become like them. It's a fact that, when you focus your emotions on someone, you tend to become like that person. Leave it to Satan, to pull us into this sinful trap. In (Romans 8:10-11) it says, "And if Christ be in you, the body is dead because of sin, but the spirit is life because of righteousness." In (Verse 11) it says, "But if the spirit of Him that raised up Jesus from the dead dwell in you, He that raised up Christ from the dead shall also quicken your mortal bodies by His Spirit that dwelleth in you."

4-Bitterness affects our relationship with God. When we pray the Lord's Prayer, we are saying something like this, "Forgive us our trespasses as we forgive those who trespass against us." When you pray this, you are saying, "God, please forgive me of my sins, just like I forgive other people of their sins against me." If you don't forgive other people, you are actually asking God not to forgive you. *Forgiveness Sets Us Free.*

This is the first step in the healing process. The only thing that can set us free, from resentment and bitterness is, forgiveness. Let me say this, "not many people truly understand what forgiveness, is." Forgiveness is'nt trying to overlook sin or pretend that it never happened. Forgiveness isn't trying to forget. Forgetting comes after forgivness, *not before*.

Okay, what's forgiveness? This is so important to understand. Forgiveness is bearing the wrong or injury yourself, and choosing to remember it no more. Forgiveness means, that you give the person who has wronged you, a clean slate. Forgiveness is costly. The one who forgives *Pays The Price* of the injury or evil that he forgives. In order for Christ to forgive us, He had to *PayThe Penalty* of our sins. This is why He died on the cross. It's costly to forgive, but it's more costly not to forgive. You may remember a certain injury or offense, that happened to you a long time ago. You may be thinking of it right, now. That person, may have indeed done you a great injustice, but that injury didn't do you, nearly the harm, you have done to yourself, by holding on to that resentment.

How do we turn from bitterness to forgiveness? The following four steps will help us, on how we can give up our bitterness:

1-Recognize that God is the judge. Yes, people need to be judged for their wrong deeds, but *You* and I, are not the ones to judge, them. Judgment belongs to God the Bible says, in (Romans 12:19-21) "Dearly beloved, avenge not yourselves, but rather give place unto wrath, for it's written, vengeance is mine, I will repay, saideth the Lord." In, (Verse 20) it says, "Therefore if thine enemy hunger, feed him, if he thirsts, give him drink, for in so doing thou shalt heap coals of fire on his head." In, (Verse 21) it says, "Be not overcome of evil, but overcome evil with good." God tells us, not to try to "get even." Or to avenge ourselves, but rather to forgive, when we forgive someone, we're turning that person over to God, recognizing that He, alone has the right to judge and punish people for their wrongdoings.

2- Confess your sins to God. A person may have done you a wrong. If so, he's responsible to God for this. But, if you are holding on to bitterness, you are sinning, and you're responsible to God for your sin of bitterness. To deal with this sin, you must confess it to God and ask Him to cleanse, you with the precious blood of His Son.

3- Pass the sentence of death upon resentment and bitterness. Resentment and bitterness are of *All Sins*. We must pass the sentence of death upon them or they'll pass the sentence of death upon us. Holding bitterness is "living after the flesh", and the Bible says, "If ye live after the flesh, ye shall die." Because we were crucified with Christ, we have the right to refuse anything, that belongs to the old life. This means, that we can refuse and reject the sin of bitterness. We have the right to ask the Lord, to put it to death by His Spirit. Now, let us pray, *"Dear Lord Jesus, I was crucified with you. Because of this, I have the right to refuse any kind of sin that belongs to my old life. Right now, I refuse and reject this resentment and all this bitterness, and I ask you, by your Holy Spirit, to put it to death. Forgive me, Lord for all my sins, and give me a forgiving heart in your precious name. I thank you, Lord, right here and right now. Your will be done. Amen and Amen!*

4-Forgive, even as Christ has forgiven you. Forgiveness involves a choice on our part. We must *Choose* to forgive. We may not *Feel* like forgiving the other person, but God, deals with our choices, not our feeling. You may ask yourself, "suppose that person doesn't ask for forgiveness or doesn't even admit that he was wrong?" How can I forgive him?

As far, as we know from the scriptures, no one ever came to Jesus and asked to be forgiven of their sins. Yet, Jesus did forgive people. He, forgave them in a very special way. He forgave them *Unilaterally*. The word unilateral, looks and sounds like a very difficult word, but it's really not that hard to understand. It means "one sided." To forgive someone unilaterally, means that you forgive from your side, regardless of what he/she has done. He/she may not ask for forgiveness, he/she may not even know, that he/she needs to be forgiven. But you can choose to forgive them anyway. The ones who crucified the Lord Jesus didn't ask for forgiveness, but Jesus forgave them anyway. He prayed "Father, forgive them for they know not what they do." Forgiveness, flowed from His heart to those who didn't ask for it or deserve it. This was unilateral forgiveness. This is the level, in which our lives should be at. When we came to the Lord for Salvation, we didn't confess every sin, that we had ever committed. We didn't ask His forgiveness for each sin. Yet, our Lord Jesus, received us and forgave us, of *Every Sin* we had ever committed.

Now, He commands us to forgive others, even as He forgave us. The Bible says, in (Colossians 3:12-17) "Put on therefore, as the elect of God, Holy and beloved, bowels of mercies, kindness, humbleness of mind, meekness, longsuffering." In (Verse 13) it says, "Forbearing one another, and forgiving one another, if any man have a quarrel against any, even as Christ forgave you, so also do ye." In (Verse 14) it says, "And above all these things put on charity, which is the bond of perfectness." In (Verse 15) it says, "And let the peace of God rule in your hearts, to which also ye are called in one body, and be ye thankful." In (Verse 16) it says, "Let the Word of Christ dwell in you richly in all wisdom, teaching and admonishing one another in psalms and hymns and spiritual songs, singing with grace in your hearts to the Lord." In (Verse 17) it says, "And whatsoever ye do in word or deed, do all in the name of the Lord Jesus, giving thanks to *God* and the Father by Him."

Let's go ahead and read on, in (Colossians 3:18-25) "Wives, submit yourselves unto your own husbands, as it is fit in the Lord." In (Verse 19) it says, "Husbands, love your wives, and be not bitter against them." In (Verse 20) it says, "Children, obey your parents in all things, for this is well pleasing unto the Lord." In (Verse 21) it says, "Fathers, provoke not your children to anger, lest they be discouraged." In (Verse 22) it says, "Servants, obey in all things your masters according to the flesh, not with eye service, as man pleasers, but in singleness of heart, fearing God." In (Verse 23) it says, "And whatsoever ye do, do it heartily, as to the Lord, and not unto men." In

(Verse 24) it says, "Knowing that of the Lord ye shall receive the reward of the inheritance, for ye serve the Lord Christ." In (Verse 25) it says, "But he that doeth wrong shall receive for the wrong which he hath done, and there is no respect of person." Although, the other person my not ask for forgiveness or even admit that he was wrong, you can still forgive. You can forgive *Unialterally*.

5- Trust the Holy Spirit to make your forgiveness *Real*. Forgiving others and getting rid, of bitterness and resentment, is the result of our working together with the Holy Spirit. We can't do it by ourselves and the Holy Spirit won't do it apart from our choice. We must work together with Him. *We Choose It, And We Trust HIM To Do It*. The Bible says, in (Romans 8:12-14) "Therefore, brethren, we are debtors, not to the flesh, to live after the flesh." In (Verse 13) it says, "For if ye live after the flesh, ye shall die, but if ye through the Spirit do mortify the deeds of the body, ye shall live." In (Verse 14) it says, "For as many as are led by the Spirit of God, they are the sons of God." We must ask, the Holy Spirit to enable us, to forgive and forget! We can "forgive" someone and then repeatedly "reinstate" their sin by dwelling on it. By *refusing* to forget it, we keep the resentment alive. May God enable us to forgive, as He forgives, to *Forgive And Forget*.

Your Way is Not God's Way

God says, in (Hebrews 8:10-13) "For this is the covenant that I will make with the house of Israel after those days, saith the Lord, I will put my laws into their mind, and write them in their hearts, and I'll be to them a God, and they shall be to me a people." In (Verse 11) it says, "And they shall not teach every man his neighbor, and every man his brother, saying, know the Lord, for all shall know me, from the least to the greatest." In (Verse 12) it says, "For I will be merciful to their unrighteousness, and their sins and their iniquities will I remember no more." In (Verse 13) it says, "In that he saith, a new covenant, he hath made the first old. Now that which decayeth and waxeth old is ready to vanish away."

An important part of turning from bitterness, to forgiveness is dealing with our feelings. We can choose to forgive and mean it, with all our heart, but the hurt is still there. To be fully free from resentment and bitterness, we must deal with our feelings. Is there a way in which we can deal with our feelings? Oh yes, there is! The way to deal with our feelings, is to change the way we look at a matter at hand. We can't change the *Facts* of a past situation, but we can change the way we *Look* at the matter. Remember, we're controlled by the way we inwardly see and believe things to be.

Consider Joseph, we have already seen how Joseph's brothers hated him, and sold him as a slave, the facts of the situation couldn't be changed. What had happened, had happened, forever. Yet Joseph wasn't resentful toward his brothers. How did Joseph manage, to have good feelings toward his brothers after all they had done to him? He put a proper *Meaning* on those circumstances. He saw God's hand in all that had happened to him. He realized, that God had used all those circumstances for his good. He said, to his brothers "you thought evil against me, but God meant it unto good!" Our "evils" are never the happenings in themselves, but the effects we allow them to have on us.

To the one who fears and doubts, all is evil. To the one who trusts, all Is Good. The story of Joseph, teaches us this great truth. God can bring good, out of a bad situation, if we trust Him. God doesn't cause evil, but He can use it, to bring about His purpose. The Bible says, in (Romans 8:27-28) "And he that searcheth the hearts knoweth what is the mind of the Spirit, because He maketh intercession for the saints according to the will of God." In (Verse 28) it says, "And we know that all things work together for good to them that love God, to them who are called according to His purpose." Notice, that in (Verse 28) it doesn't say that we "see" or that we "understand," but that, "we know that all things work together for good to them that love God." We may not see or understand how all things, are working together for our good, but we can, for sure, know it because, *God Says So*.

Now, concerning our situation we can't change the facts, what has happened, has happened, and we can't change it. But, we can trust God, to bring good out of the situation. We can say, "Lord, what that person did, seems bad to me," but you said, "that all things work together for good to them that love you."

I believe you to bring good out of this, just as you did in Joseph's case. When we believe that God, is using all things, even those things which seem bad to us, for our eternal good, we see things in a different way. As you can see, "**Your Way is Not God's Way**." We can actually, thank God, for the things that happened to us. This takes the hurt out of the past offenses and *Sets Us Free* from resentment and bitterness. Concerning those who have wronged us, we can say, with Joseph, "you brought evil against me, but God meant it unto good." Remember this, resentment and bitterness can and will make prisoners of us, but *Forgiveness Sets Us Free*. Now, we can say, "*God's way is our way.*"

In prayer, thank the Lord, that your old self was crucified with Christ, so that you no longer have to be a slave to sin, including the sin of a quick temper. Heavenly Father, I thank you, for the strength of your Grace. I thank you, for coming near to me and lifting me up. You know, it took time to change old habits, but God will faithfully help you, as you obey His Word.

Chapter 25

The Lord, has spoken to me about, His children about giving. There's, three great principles regarding money and possessions:

1-God owns all things.
2-All things come from God.
3-We, and all that we have belonged to, God.

God requires, that we give the first 10% to Him. This is called tithing. It means "the tenth." It's very simple to understand, if we make a hundred dollars, 10% of that is, ten dollars. For each dollar, the Lord gets a dime. The purpose of tithing, is to remind us, of God's ownership of all things and to teach us, to put God first, in our lives. He teaches this in the Old Testament and the New Testament. God's exceedingly generous. He allowed, them to keep nine-tenths, of all that they produced, but the tithe, or the tenth, belonged to Him. The Bible says, in (Leviticus 27:30) "And all the tithe of the land, whether of the seed of the land or of the fruit, of the tree, is the Lord's, it is Holy unto the Lord." In, addition to their tithes, God's people gave free will, offerings. The tithes and offerings, were given to the priests of God. God's people, were told to bring their tithes and offerings, when they came to worship God. God said, in (Deuteronomy 16:16-17) "Three times in a year shall all thy males appear before the Lord thy God in the place which He shall choose, in the feast of unleavened bread, and in the feast of weeks, and in the feast of tabernacles, and they shall not appear before the Lord empty." In (Verse 17) it says, "Every man shall give as he is able, according to the blessing of the Lord thy God which he hath given thee." God was teaching His people to give. When they gave freely to God, He gave them an abundant crop.

The Bible says, in (Proverbs 3:9-10) it says, "Honor the Lord with thy substance, and with the firstfruits of all thine increase." In (Verse 10) it says, "So shall thy barns be filled with plenty, and thy presses shall burst out with new wine." Were God's people, in the Old Testament, always faithful, in giving their tithes and offering to Him? No, they weren't. God said, in (Malachi 3:8) "Will a man rob God? Yet ye have robbed Me. But ye say, wherein have we robbed Thee? In tithes and offering." What happened when they robbed God? They came under God's chastening hand. God said, in (Malachi 3:9) "Ye are cursed with a curse, for ye have robbed me, even this whole nation." When God's people, repented of their disobedience and began, once again, to obey Him in the matter of tithes and offering. God, poured out His blessings upon them. God said, in (Malachi 3:10) "Bring ye all the tithes into the storehouse, that there may be meat in mine house, and prove me now herewith, saith the Lord of hosts, if I will not open you the windows of Heaven, and pour you out a blessing, that there shall not be room enough to receive it." In the New Testament, the great principle regarding giving, is this, "when we give to God, God gives to us."

The Lord Jesus said, in (Luke 6:38) "Give, and it shall be given unto you, good measure, pressed down, and shaken together, and running over, shall men give into your bosom. For with the same measure that ye mete withal it shall be measured to you again." When God gives, He, gives bountifully. He's very generous. In Jesus's time, people brought their grain in bulk. Many sellers would pour the grain into a measure, without allowing the buyer to shake it down. Not so, with the Lord, He gives "good measure pressed down, shaken together, and running over."

Giving enables God to give to us. The more we give, the more God gives to us. The less we give, the less God gives us. Jesus said, "For with the same measure ye mete (give) withal it shall be measured (given) to you again." Both, the Old and New Testaments lay down the same teaching. When we give to God, He gives to us. God's not poor, nor is He stingy, He loves to give to His children. But, we must fulfill His conditions, give and it shall be given to you. God tells us to give, because He wants His children to be like Him. God is generous, and He wants us, to be generous. Another, reason why God asks us, to give is that we might, "lay up treasure in Heaven." We can't send our money to Heaven, but we can give it, to win others to Christ. This is laying up treasure in Heaven. God's Word, gives us a number of principles regarding giving:

1-First, give yourself to God. The first gift, God wants from us, is ourselves. The order is, first give yourself to God, and then give a portion of that which God has given to you. The Christians in Macedonia, did just this, and the Apostle Paul, commended them for it. Paul wrote, in (ll Corinthians 8:5) "And this they did, not as we hoped, but first gave their own selves to the Lord, and unto us by the will of God."

2-Give as God has prospered you. In the Old Testament, God commanded His people, to give the first tenth, of all they earned to Him. In the New Testament, God hasn't laid down a law as, to how much we are to give. Instead, God's Word says, "Let everyone, of you lay by Him in a store as God has prospered him." What percentage of our income should we give? We can take the tithe (10%) as a guide to the "*Minimum*" we should give, but our giving could be much more than this. It depends on how thankful we are for the way God, has blessed us, and how strongly we desire to "lay up treasure in Heaven."

3-Give systematically. Giving is an act of worship, and our giving must not, be a hit or miss, proposition. We're to give regularly and systematically, upon the first day of the week, when we come to worship God. The Bible says, in (I Corinthians 16:2) "Upon the first day of the week let everyone of you lay by him in store, as God hath prospered him, that there be no gatherings when I come." No one is excluded. Old, young, poor, or rich, all must be involved in giving. The Bible says, "Let every one of you lay by him in store as God has prospered him."

4-Give cheerfully and liberally. Whatever, we give to the Lord, He wants us to give it out of a willing heart. God doesn't want us to give grudgingly. The Bible says, in (ll Corinthians 9:7-8) "Every man according as he purposeth in his heart, so let him give, not grudgingly, or of necessity, for God loveth a cheerful giver." In (Verse 8) it says, "And God is able to make all grace abound toward you, that ye, always having all sufficiency in all things, may abound to every good work."

5-Give wisely. The Lord Jesus said, that we're to be "good and wise stewards." Some, Christians give liberally, but they're not wise in their giving. To give to a Church or organization that's not faithfully preaching God's Word, is not wise giving. We should be as careful, in investing our Lord's money, we would be in investing in a business. We should invest it, where it will bring the greatest spiritual returns. You don't have to possess large sums of money, to be a big giver, in God's sight. God doesn't measure our giving, by the size of our gifts. He, measures our giving, by how much we give, out of what we have. God, looks at how much sacrifice, is involved in our giving. By God's way, of measuring our giving, a poor person can give as much or more than a wealthy person.

Our giving should cost us something. On one occasion, the Lord Jesus, stood at the temple watching as the people brought their gifts. Some were rich and gave more. Then a poor widow, came by and gave two small copper coins. These coins were of little monetary value, yet, in God's sight, this woman had given more than all, who gave that day. Why? Because she had given all that she had, even her "living." Jesus said, in (Mark 12:43-44) "Verily I say unto you, that this poor widow has cast more in, than all they which have cast into the treasury." In (Verse 44) it says, "For all they did cast in of their abundance, but she of her want did cast in all that she had, even all her living."

In His Word, God tells, us to whom we should give:

1-We should give to our local Churchs. Most of our gifts, normally should go to our local Church, provided that the Church is one where, the Bible is, faithfully taught and Christ is exalted. God has ordained, that His Church and His ministers be supported by the gifts of His people. The Bible says, in (I Corinthians

9:13-14) "Do ye not know that they which minister about Holy things live of the things of the temple? and they which wait at the altar are partakers with the altar?" In (Verse 14) it says, "Even so hath the Lord ordained that they which preach the Gospel should live of the Gospel."

2- We should give, to those who have helped us, spiritually. We're instructed in God's Word to share our money with those who have taught us the Word of God, and helped us spiritually. The Bible says, in (Galatians 6:6) "Let him that is taught in the Word communicatae unto him that teacheth in all good things."

3- We should give to those who are in need. This is one way in which we can show, that we have the love of God in our hearts. We find, in (I John 3:17-18) "But whoso hath this world's good, and seeth his brother have need, and shutteth up his bowels of compassion from him, how dwelleth the love of God in him?" In (Verse 18) it says, "My little children, let us not love in word, neither in tongue, but in deed and in truth." As a general rule, our giving to the needy, should be done trough the local Church. *All* of our giving, should be done simply and without, drawing any attention to ourselves. The Bible says, "He that gives let him do it simply."

4- We should give to those who are taking the Gospel to the lost. Every Christian, has a responsibility, to get the Gospel to the lost.

God's command to us is, "go ye into all the world, and preach the Gospel to every creature." If we can't go ourselves, we should count it a privilege to help support missionaries, who are taking the Gospel to those who have never, heard of Christ.

Giving is sowing. I have already written some, on sowing, but sowing is giving. Giving isn't just throwing your money, away. This, I know to be a very true fact, in my own life. When we sow a seed, we're not throwing it away, we're simply planting it, so that we may reap a harvest, later. The size of our harvest, will greatly depend on how much we planted, this is true of our giving. Writing to the Church, at Corinth, concerning giving. Paul said, in (ll Corinthians 9:6-7) "But this I say, he which soweth sparingly shall reap also sparingly, and he which soweth bountifully shall reap also bountifully." In (Verse 7) it says, "Every man according as he purposeth in his heart, so let him give, not grudgingly, or of necessity, for God loveth a cheerful giver. God, wants to provide money for the support of His Churches, and the money to send His servants, to the unreachable people of in the world." How does He do this? He gives money to us, that we may give back to His, work. He wants us to be able to give generously. In (ll Corinthians 9:8) says, "And God is able to make all grace abound toward you, that ye, always having all sufficiency in all things, may abound to every good work." The Lord Jesus, Himself is our great example in the matter of giving. In (ll Corinthians 8:9) it says, "For ye know the grace of our Lord Jesus Christ, that, though he was rich, yet for your sakes he became poor, that ye through his poverty might be rich." (Let's start making eternal friendships.)

Jesus often taught His Disciples by means of parables. A parable, is a short story, that brings out one or more spiritual truths. In (Luke 16) it says, "The Lord Jesus told of a certain rich man who had a steward, who managed his property for him. When the rich man received word, that his steward was wasting his goods, he called his steward before him, to give an account of his stewardship. When the steward realized that he would soon be out of a job, he said, to himself "what shall I do? For my master is taking the stewardship away from me. I can't beg, I'm to ashamed to beg. I have resolved what to do, that when I'm put out of the stewardship, they, (the friends, I'm going to make) may receive me into their houses." This steward, devised a plan, to provide for his future. He decided to call his masters debtors to him, and make generous settlements with them. In that way, they would become indebted to him and become his friends. Then, when he was out of a job, these friends, would receive him into their houses and provide him room and board. The steward, quickly began to carry out his plan. The Bible says, "So he called everyone of his master's debtors to him, and said to the first, "how much do you owe my master?" And, he said, "a hundred measures of oil." So, he said to him, "take your bill, and sit down quickly and write fifty." Then, he said, to another, "and how much do you owe?" So, he said, "a hundred measures of wheat." And, he said, to him, "take your bill, and write eighty." The steward did likewise with all who owed the master. Now, what was he doing? He was providing for his future. He was making friends, for the future, when he would not have a job. The master of the steward commended his steward for his shrewdness, even though it meant some loss of revenue to him. He recognized, that the steward needed to provide some security for his future.

>From this parable, the Lord would have us learn three very important principles:

1-Life is a stewardship not an ownership. All that we have belongs to, God. We don't own anything. We're simply God's servants, managing what He has entrusted to us.
2-One day we must give an account of our stewardship. God has given us life, health, talents, abilities, money, and many other things. One day, we must give an account to Him, of what we have done with what He has entrusted to us. Just to hear Him say, "well done, thou good and faithful servant" will be worth more than anything this world, has to offer.
3-The wisest, and best use of money, is using it to win others to Christ. Jesus, summed up the heart of the story with this statement, found, in (Luke 16:9) "And I say to you, make to yourselves friends, of the mammon (money) of unrighteousness that, when ye fail, they may receive you unto everlasting habitations."

What the Lord, is saying, here, is that "we're to use our money to make eternal friendships, so that these friends that we helped win for Christ, may be there, to welcome us when, we enter Heaven." Will there be anyone in Heaven to say, to you, "you are my friend, I've been waiting for you?" The day is coming when our money and riches will be useless, and meaningless. The day is coming when our stewardship will be over. In the little time we have left, we should use our money to win others to Christ. And thus make eternal friendships.

This is the wisest and best use of our money. Each of us should ask ourselves these questions, am I a good steward, of all that God has entrusted to me? Am I using my money to make eternal friends? Will there be anyone to greet me in Heaven and say, to me, "if it hadn't been for you, I would'nt be in this wonderful, beautiful place."

The question is, "are you on the right road?" How are you going to Heaven? Which road are you traveling? The world teaches us, that all roads lead to Heaven, that it doesn't matter which Church you attend, as long as you go to Church. Is this the right road? Let's see what God's Word, has to say about the road to Heaven. In (John 14:6-7) it says, "Jesus saith unto Him, I am the way, the truth, and the life, no man cometh unto the Father, but by Me." In (Verse 7) it says "If ye had known Me, ye should have known my Father also, and from henceforth ye know Him, and have seen Him." Jesus didn't say, there're many ways, only one way to Heaven. In (Acts 16:17) it says, "The same followed Paul and us, and cried, saying, these men are the servants of the most high God, which shew unto us the way of Salvation."

If you're on the wrong road, it's leading you straight to Hell. You must make a choice in your life. Is it Heaven or Hell? In (Romans 3:10) it says, "As it is written, there is none righteous, no, not one." That applies to you and me. In (Romans 3:23) it says, "For all have sinned, and come short of the Glory of God." In (Romans 6:23) it says, "For the wages of sin is death, but the gift of God is eternal life through Jesus Christ our Lord." Because of sin in your life, you can't go to Heaven, unless you go through our Lord Jesus Christ. What will it be for you?

In (Romans 5:8) says, "But God commendeth His love toward us, in that, while we were yet sinners, Christ died for us." In (Romans 10:9) it says, "That if thou shalt confess with thy mouth the Lord Jesus, and shalt believe in thine heart that God hath raised Him from the dead, thou shalt be saved." The only way to be on the right road to Heaven, is to receive the Lord Jesus, into your heart. In (Romans 10:13) it says, "For whosoever shall call upon the name of the Lord shall be *Saved*."

In (Ephesians 2:8-9) it says, "For by grace are ye saved through faith, and not that of yourselves, it is a gift of God." In (Verse 9) it says, "Not of works, lest any man should boast." God's Word says, in (II Corinthians 6:2) "For He saith, I have heard thee in a time accepted, and in the day of Salvation have I succoured thee, behold, now is the excepted time, behold, now is the day of Salvation." Don't put it

Your Way is Not God's Way

off, as the time is very important. We don't know if we have another day to live.

In (James 4:14) it says, "Whereas ye know not what shall be on the morrow. For what is your life? It is even a vapour, that appeareth for a little time, and then vanisheth away." Where will you be tomorrow? Is today, your last time to accept Christ, before it's too late? In (Hebrews 9:27) it says, "And as it is appointed unto men once to die, but after this the judgment." In (Hebrews 9:28) it says, "So Christ was once offered to bear the sins of many, and unto them that look for Him shall He appear the second time without sin unto Salvation." All of mankind must leave this world one day. We don't know the day or the hour, but we can be ready.

Is today your day, for you? In (Revelation 3:20-22) it says, "Behold, I stand at the door, and knock, if any man hear my voice, and open the door, I will come in to him, and will sup with him, and he with Me." In (Verse 21) it says, "To him that overcometh will I grant to sit with Me in my throne, even as I also overcame, and am set down with my Father in His throne." In (Verse 22) it says, "He that hath an ear, let him hear what the spirit saith unto the Churches." Even now, Jesus is speaking to you from His Word. Would you please accept Him as your Savior? As a lost sinner, if you were to die today, you would go to Hell? You're not able to save yourself, not even by good works, nor by living a good life, or by going to Church. There's only one way, Jesus said, "*I Am The Way, The Truth, And The Life.*" **YOUR WAY IS**

NOT GOD'S WAY. What will you do? If you refuse Jesus, you're on the wrong road.

I feel the need to pray, please pray with me this prayer, *"Dear Jesus, I come to you, my heart is heavy with sin. I'm here right now, asking you to forgive me of all my sins. And to come into my heart and save me. I want to be in that number, when you come back to take your children home. Dear God, some of the greatest lessons, we learn, are only after our hearts have suffered. God in times of pain, we receive wisdom, and in times of sorrow, we gain understanding. Father, this is your way of teaching our hearts, that we must know darkness, in order to embrace your light. Thank you for saving me, and for being our compassionate teacher."* Lord in your Word, in (Psalms 145:18-20) it says, "The Lord is nigh unto all them that call upon Him, to all that call on Him in truth. In (Verse 19) it says, "He will fulfil the desire of them that fear Him, He also will hear their cry, and will saves them." In (Verse 20) it says, "The Lord preserveth all them that love Him, but all the wicked willl be destroy." We praise you, Lord, for eternal life. And we thank you for your love for each one of us. It is done, right now in the name of Jesus. Amen and Amen.

Thank you Lord Jesus, for dying on the cross for our sins. I can't wait to meet each one of you in Heaven, in God's wonderful reunion. As, I bring this book to a close, it's my desire to leave you feeling complete, satisfied, and fulfilled.

I don't want you to fill empty and continue looking for something to fill the emptiness, that will only add to the pain, you may already be experiencing. You must know who you are in, Jesus. You must understand your righteousness, (your right standing with God), is found only in Christ. Everything you need is available for the taking. All you have to do, is receive by faith, what Jesus has already provided, let faith take the lead in your life, and your feelings will follow. First, you must believe that God loves you, affirm it to yourself daily through prayer, meditating on it, and by speaking of it. Your feelings will come along, later.

Start believing you have been made acceptable in Jesus. Ask, Him for favor with the right people. The Bible says, "You have not, because you ask not." And don't worry about all the others, who don't seem to value you. They're the ones that are missing out, because actually you are a great person, and God loves you. The relationship with you, and God, is something to be greatly desired. Live to please God, you have His approval and that's all you really need. I believe God's doing something wonderful in you and will continue to do something wonderful through, you.

Your critics, may live to see the day, when they wish they had treated you better, while you were still in the process of "becoming" all that God, wants you to be. Because through God, all things are possible. Meditate on your position, in Christ according to God's Word. Jesus endured horrible pain, as He hung on the cross, paying for our sins. But, His pain is our gain.

Your Way is Not God's Way

God's Word teaches us, that when we don't know how to pray, as we should in a situation, the Holy Spirit comes to our aide. He knows the will of the Father in all things, and pleads in behalf of all the Saints, according to and in harmony with God's will. Therefore we can be assured and know that all things work together for good, for those who love God, and are called according to His purposes. No, matter what happens in life, if we'll keep praying and trusting God, keep loving Him and walking in His will to the best of our ability. He'll cause everything, to work out for the good! Whatever happened, to us in the past, may not have been good in and of itself, and it may have led us to a lot of struggles. But, because God is good, He can take a very difficult and painful situation and cause it to work out for our good, and the good of others.

We wonder sometimes, why God waits so long to come to our rescue, or why He allows certain things to happen or take place. We can't always figure out, what God's doing or why, He's doing it, but if we *Trust* and *Obey* Him, He'll make something wonderful from it. *Always remember...* **"Your Way is Not God's Way!"** GOD'S WAY, IS OUR WAY, TO HEAVEN. Amen!

Printed in the United States
204746BV00001B/106-1176/P